GOING LIVE

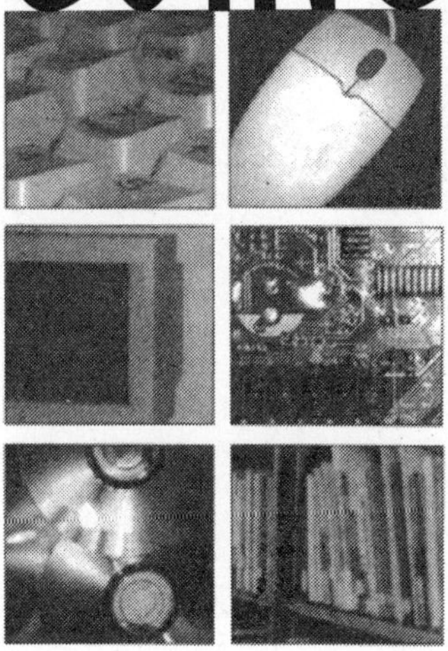

Starting & Running a Virtual Reference Service

STEVE COFFMAN

with contributions by Michelle Fiander, Kay Henshall, and Bernie Sloan

AMERICAN LIBRARY ASSOCIATION
Chicago

In Association With

Ess Ess Publications
New Delhi

Going Live:
Starting and Running a Virtual Reference Service

 Published by **Ess Ess Publications**, 4837/24, Ansari Road, Darya Ganj, New Delhi-110 002, India, in arrangement with **American Library Association**, 50, East Huron Street, Chicago, Illinios 60611, United States of America.

ISBN: 978-81-7000-578-0

Rs.700/-

First Indian Imprint 2009

Published by:
Ess Ess Publications
4837/24, Ansari Road,
Darya Ganj,
New Delhi-110 002.
INDIA
Phones: 23260807, 41563444
Fax: 41563334
E-mail: info@essessreference.com
www.essessreference.com

in arrangement with

American Library Association
50, East Huron Street,
Chicago, Illinios 60611
United States of America

Printed and bound in India at Salasar Imaging Systems.

CONTENTS

PREFACE *v*

CHAPTER ONE
Reference: The First One Hundred Years *1*

CHAPTER TWO
Getting Started: Designing Virtual Reference Systems *22*

CHAPTER THREE
Managing Virtual Reference Services *48*

CHAPTER FOUR
Marketing Virtual Reference Services *73*

CHAPTER FIVE
Where Do We Go from Here? *90*

APPENDIXES
A Software Feature Checklist *107*
B Sample Pre-employment Screening Test and Key *146*

VIRTUAL REFERENCE SERVICES BIBLIOGRAPHY *157*
by Bernie Sloan

INDEX *177*

PREFACE

I remember when I first laid eyes on virtual reference. It was back in 1997 and I was trying to round up speakers for the SCOUG's (the infamous Southern California Online Users Group—for those of you who may be new to the field) spring workshop on new reference technologies. Chris Ferguson, then the head of the Leavey Library at the University of Southern California (USC), suggested that Lucent Technologies had some things that might be interesting and put me in touch with Bob Kent, who was then USC's personal Lucent customer services rep. Bob invited me down to one of the Lucent Demonstration Centers for lunch and began to show off all kinds of new gadgets, electronics, and technologies that might possibly have some applications for reference. There were miniature wireless headsets like the Secret Service wears that would allow librarians to work with patrons on the phone and roam the stacks at the same time. There were IVR (integrated voice response) systems that might be used to answer routine questions automatically without human intervention. There were knowledge bases and CRM (customer relationship management) software packages that might allow us to track what patrons were asking and capture the most common questions and answers so we would never have to answer them again. There were call routing systems that could handle thousands of questions per minute, and make sure they were all sent to librarians with the right skill set to answer them . . . provided, of course, the patron pushed the right button. And there was call center software that integrated the telephone and the computer so that agents could answer their phone by clicking a button on the screen, and the customer record and other information the agent needed to answer the question would be automatically pulled up on the computer.

I told Kent it was all very interesting, but there was one pretty serious limitation. It was all based on the telephone, and although libraries certainly offered telephone reference . . . the telephone was designed primarily for talking and is certainly not the most effective method of sharing large amounts of information and content online. That's why we invented the Web. "Ah ha," Kent said, "then I have just the thing for you," and he pointed out a couple of computers on the other side of the room. On one there was a mock-up of the Lucent website with a link that said "Have a Question? Click Here to Ask Me," and it showed a picture of a call center agent. The other computer had the agent's interface, which looked a lot like the call center software I had seen earlier, but this thing was also designed to accept "web calls." Customers who clicked on Lucent's "Ask Me" button would be routed to agents in the call center just like a phone call . . . only now, the agent could "push" information from the Web to the customers' browser window, and guide them around the Lucent site or anywhere else on the Web using something called "co-browsing" technology. If the customer had a free line, they could talk with the agent on the phone while using the computer for co-browsing; otherwise they could communicate with "chat." Although many of the functions were pretty rudimentary in comparison with some of the sophisticated virtual reference software we have nowadays, I thought I could see in that early collaboration program the core of a new technology that could allow libraries to move their reference services to the Web—if libraries could only be convinced to take advantage of it. I figured it couldn't hurt to give things a little push in that direction, so I invited Bob up to show off the collaboration program at SCOUG—and it's all been downhill from there.

A whole lot has happened in the six years since I had that meeting with Bob Kent. I'm not sure what happened to Bob, but Lucent Technologies, which was flying high at the time, got caught in the dot.com and telecommunications implosion, and is now but a shadow of its former self. Its stock, which had been trading for over seventy-five dollars a share, is now going for little more than one dollar. And the real irony is that I don't think they ever sold a single one of their web collaboration packages to libraries. In the same period, we've witnessed the birth—and then the death—of dozens and dozens of commercial reference services that aimed to replace libraries on the Web. Remember how worried we were when WebHelp introduced its live, free web reference services, and its CEO, Kerry Adler, said that his "Web Wizards" were going to be the new "librarians of cyberspace"? Well, WebHelp is still around, but it has "repurposed" itself to focus on BPO, or business process outsourcing . . .

which is a far cry from live web reference services, and those Web Wizards are nowhere to be found. And Mr. Jeeves and most of the other "question-answering" services have suffered similar fates.

As for libraries . . . they've embraced virtual reference with open arms. Back when I met with Lucent in 1997, the first interactive reference service had just gotten started at the State University of New York at Morrisville . . . and all it could do was chat. There was no page-pushing or co-browsing, or any of the other interactive features we've come to rely on. Today, Library Systems and Services, LLC (LSSI) alone provides virtual reference softwarc for several thousand libraries all over the world, and when you add in the libraries supported by all the other vendors now crowding into this field . . . there are probably now more than 4,000 libraries that offer live online reference services of one sort or another. And libraries are launching new services so rapidly that it is almost impossible to keep an accurate count. The technology has also evolved from "just chat" to full web collaboration, including file and application sharing, database authentication, and in some cases, even voice and video over the Internet.

In the beginning, none of us knew the first thing about how to start and run a virtual reference service, so we just made it up as we went along. At first we made a lot of mistakes—like the ten-minute rule, initially instituted by the QandACafe service in northern California, that said web reference sessions would have to be limited to no more than ten minutes in order to help the librarians handle the thousands of people who they were sure would log in as soon as the service opened. Of course, we learned that we hardly needed to worry about being overwhelmed, and that the real problem was getting enough people to log in to our services to begin with . . . not how to restrict the amount of time we spent with those who were lucky enough to find us. But we have learned a lot in the past few years. Each library that's started a new service has added a bit to our understanding and taught us a little more about how to handle virtual reference. The problem is that up until now most of that knowledge was locked up inside people's heads, and the only way to get it was to call around and try to interview as many "virtual reference veterans" as possible.

That is a hard way to learn about anything, and so this book is an attempt to collect and document what we have learned about virtual reference in the past few years, to help make it easier for all of you who are coming after us. The information presented here is based on our collective experience at LSSI in helping to design and develop several hundred virtual reference projects involving thousands of libraries of all types in countries all over the world.

I am especially indebted to Michelle Fiander and Kay Henshall, who contributed significant portions of chapter 3 and who helped me better understand how librarians and patrons were actually using the technology; and to Bernie Sloan for contributing his great "Virtual Reference Services Bibliography," for all of the work he has done documenting the growth of virtual reference over these first tumultuous years, and for asking some really good questions. Finally, even though our names are on the title page, in a very real sense, this book is by each and every one of the thousands of you who have worked so hard to build and run virtual reference services all over the world. Some of you have spoken or written about it, others have posted to discussion lists, still others have designed systems or drafted RFPs, but many of you have simply worked hard to use this new technology to provide the very best reference service you could. Each of you—in his or her own way—has worked to make virtual reference what it is today. And if it were not for all of you, and the work you have done, the problems you have solved, and the frustrations you have endured, virtual reference would not exist and neither would this book.

But the story is not finished yet. We've all worked hard to get virtual reference off the ground in the past few years, but there are still many questions and issues to be resolved before we know whether we truly have what it takes to move reference to the Web, or whether these services we've fought so hard to launch will eventually wither away and die like those commercial services that preceded us. We still don't know what would happen if libraries went all out to market their virtual reference services, or how they would handle the traffic if they did. We don't really know how we are going to staff these services or how we will fund them when our grants run out. And there are complicated and difficult questions that have arisen around issues like patron privacy, copyright, library cooperation, reference quality, security, and a host of others. These chapters have yet to be written, and nobody is quite sure yet how all of this might end. The only thing we can be sure of is that this is no time to rest on our laurels. If we are to succeed it will require the same vision, dedication, and just plain hard work it took to get these services started in the first place. For all of our efforts, virtual reference is still very much a work in progress. Now let's get going, for there is much to be done.

CHAPTER ONE

Reference

The First One Hundred Years

Reference used to be such a stable and predictable area of library practice.

For much of the rest of the library profession, the past few decades have been quite a wild ride. In the 1960s the development of the Online Computer Library Center (OCLC) and cooperative cataloging revolutionized the art of bibliographic control . . . and the lives of many catalogers. The advent of automated circulation systems radically changed the way we keep track of our collections and drastically reduced the number of staff we needed to perform these operations. The development of new automated acquisitions and serials control software has changed the lives of many bibliographers and serials librarians.

But for the longest time, it seemed as if reference librarians were missing out on all this excitement.

When I first set foot behind a reference desk in 1985, reference had changed very little from what Samuel Swett Green had described when he first launched reference librarianship more than a century earlier. When I started, as in Green's time, people came to the library because it was the single most important information source in the community. If a person had a question that could not be answered by a friend or in an encyclopedia or almanac they might have about the house, they had no choice but to come and ask us—or go without knowing altogether. Of course, we didn't always make it too easy for them to ask us. The library was only open during selected hours, so if you were unlucky enough to have a question in the middle of the night or on a weekend, you often had to wait until the next business day to ask it. And if you had any kind of a question at all, we normally made you come down and ask it at the reference desk, so there was the added hassle of driving to the library, finding a parking space, waiting in line at the desk, and other minor irritations. But back in those days we were the only game in town, and if you really wanted an answer to your question, you had to be willing to put up with it.

Reference practice, too, had remained largely unchanged over the years. Reference librarians generally sat behind reference desks (although Green had actually recommended that they mingle with the readers), and when a patron came up with a question, we would first interview them to determine what they actually wanted, and then use our knowledge of reference sources and the local collection to help the patron find what they needed. If the answer was not to be found in our collections, we usually tried to refer the patron to another likely source. In academic libraries, we tended to focus on teaching the student the process so they might learn to do the research on their own, while in public and corporate libraries, we generally focused on getting the answer and spared the patron the lesson. But the basic process was still the same and had remained so for more than 100 years.

Of course, reference work has not been totally static. We have incorporated a few new technologies over the years. In the 1930s many libraries began to offer telephone reference, so that patrons with brief questions could call us up and ask them rather than come down to the library. It is interesting to note that the development of the telephone and especially the 800 number truly revolutionized question-answering and customer service in many industries, including airlines, banking, retail, and a host of others. But the telephone is not an ideal technology for sharing large amounts of information, particularly information printed in books. So although the telephone has made it easier for some patrons to reach us in some cases, it has largely been relegated to ready reference purposes and did not have the impact on library reference services that it had in other industries.

In the 1970s libraries began to add online databases to their reference toolkit, but here again, this was an incremental change that did not fundamentally alter the way we do our work. Online databases were expensive and complex, and in most cases, patrons needed a librarian's assistance to use them effectively. And as long as the patron had to come down to the library to use the database or ask the reference librarian's assistance to search it, the effect was that of adding a new source to the reference collection, while the basic reference process remained unaltered. Searches in online databases might be much faster than they had been in printed indexes and abstracts, and the new Boolean logic might have helped turn up citations that would have been difficult to find before, but the role of the reference librarian and the basic reference process remained unchanged, regardless of whether the librarian was using books or new electronic resources to help the patron find the answer.

In fact, with a little training on telephone etiquette, keyboarding, Boolean logic, and modern-day usage, there is no doubt that Samuel Swett Green himself could have been dropped behind my reference desk in 1985 and felt right at home. Many other aspects of the library were changing radically and quickly, but reference was not one of them. By 1985 we had been doing reference work pretty much the same way for over 100 years, and the role of the librarian, the patron, and the process of answering questions would have been as familiar to Green as when he was sitting behind the desk at Worcester, Massachusetts, back in 1875. But all of that was about to change.

THE INTERNET AND REFERENCE SERVICES

Beginning in the mid-1990s, the Internet that had been poking along for decades as an esoteric research network suddenly caught the popular imagination with the development of the World Wide Web. Companies, trade associations, government agencies, colleges and universities, and thousands of just plain folk rushed to build their own websites, and the content they built into them included everything from snapshots of the family dog and cat to articles, reports, statistics, graphs; every conceivable kind of gray literature; enormous catalogs like Amazon.com and the Internet Movie Database; audio and video clips; the full text of newspapers and periodicals, encyclopedias, almanacs, and many books; and much, much more. Search engines were developed to help people find the information they were seeking among the millions of sites proliferating on the Web. People bought computers by the truckload, and Internet service providers like America Online (AOL) and hundreds of others emerged to help give those computers access to the Web. Within the space of a few short years, the Internet had been transformed into an enormous online information bazaar that seemed to offer at least some information on almost any question a person could think of. And the library and library reference services, which for years had been the only game in town, suddenly had some tough competition.

Now, if you had a question, you had a real choice. You could either go down to the library and ask your question at the reference desk, or . . . you could simply get on your computer, type your question in one of the many search engines, and see what the Internet had to offer. Of course, if you chose the library, it meant you'd have to make sure it was open, then you'd have to get dressed, drive down there, find a parking space, stand in line at the reference desk, spend some time working with the librarian, and maybe you'd eventually leave with the information you needed, depending on the kind of question you asked and the resources of the library you used. The Internet, on the other hand, is open all hours of the day and night; you could use it right from the comfort of your home or office, even in your pajamas if you wanted to. You didn't have to worry about driving or parking, or trying to explain your question to somebody else. All you had to do was type it in a search engine, and results would come back immediately. And as the wealth of information on the Internet grew, there was always a good chance you would come up with something on your question. For some questions, in fact, the results were much better than you could find in almost any library (searches on current news or topics too esoteric to be covered in most library collections, for example), and even when the question might have been better answered in a library, many people found the resources on the Internet "plenty good enough" in comparison with the hassle of doing a more thorough search with traditional methods.

Small wonder, then, that increasing numbers of people are finding it more convenient to go to the Internet to look for information than to go to the library. And they are going to the Internet in a big way. If you take a look at the most recent figures from Search Engine Watch, there are now almost as many searches being done each day on just a few of the most popular Internet search engines (a total of 301 million daily searches for Google, AltaVista, Inktomi, DirectHit, FAST, GoTo, and Ask Jeeves) as the total number of reference questions asked in a full year in all U.S. public and academic libraries combined (309.6 million searches per year).[1]

And as more people have been going to the Internet, fewer have been coming to our libraries. If you look at library reference statistics over the past few years, it is not hard to see that much of the increase in Internet traffic has been matched by a similar decline in library traffic. The most current reference statistics in our field are from the Association of

Research Libraries (ARL), and if you compare the ARL reference statistics (see figure 1-1) with Nielsen figures on the total U.S. population on the Web (see figure 1-2), you see almost a mirror image.[2] As the total U.S. population on the Web began to grow significantly starting in 1997, the total number of questions asked at ARL libraries began a steady decline from a high of 158,000 in 1997 to a low of 117,000 in 2000, the latest year for which figures are available. That is a 26-percent drop in just four years, and the trend shows no sign of leveling off.

Comprehensive statistics for public libraries are not as current, but anecdotal evidence from a variety of sources indicates that the decline in the number of reference questions asked at many public libraries is just as severe as what we see in the ARL statistics. For example, Terry Casey, a trustee of the Columbus (Ohio) Public Library Board (and a marketing researcher by day), recently conducted a study where he asked a random sample of the Columbus population what source they used first when they needed information. (See figure 1-3.) Casey ran the study twice, once in December 1998 and again in June 2000. In that eighteen-month period he

FIGURE 1-1 ARL reference statistics, 1997–2000

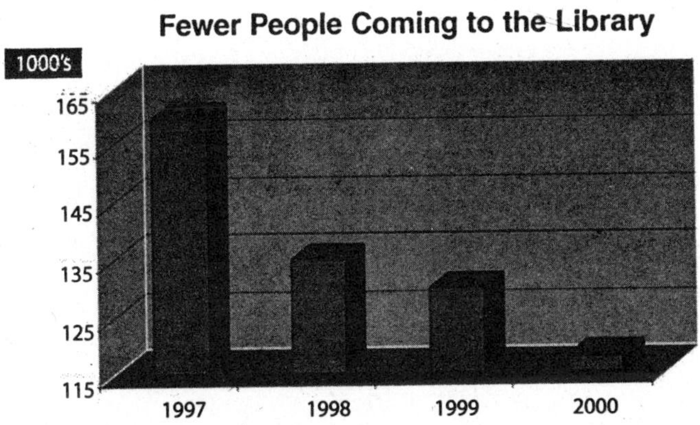

Reference statistics for all ARL libraries
Service trends in ARL libraries, 1991–2000

FIGURE 1-2 U.S. population on the Web, 1995–2001

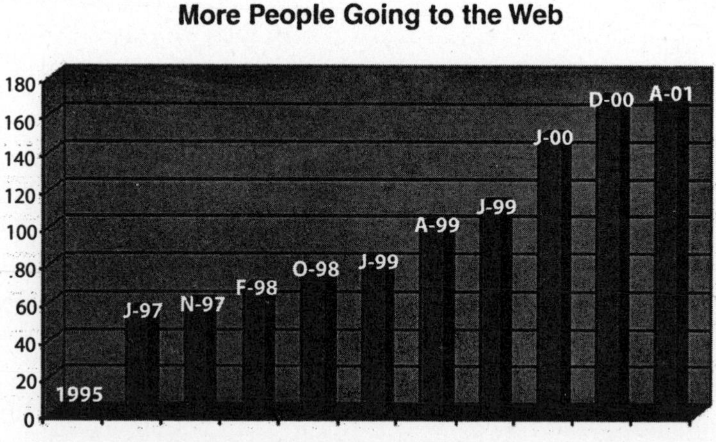

People on the Net in the United States, 1995–2001 (Nielsen and others)

FIGURE 1-3 Where people turn first for information. Courtesy of Terry Casey, ALTA (Association for Library Trustees and Advocates) presentation at the American Library Association's Annual Conference, July 7, 2000, Chicago

Information Sources	December 1998	June 2000
Internet	22.8	35.7
Books	14.6	12.3
Library	24.3	12.3
Friends	8.4	9.0

found that those who said they used the Internet first increased from 22.8 percent to 35.7 percent, while those that reported going to the library first dropped from 24.3 percent to 12.3 percent. Again, in a mirror image, almost the entire increase in people using the Internet seemed to come from an equal decrease in those using the library.

These figures are reinforced by recent postings on some reference discussion lists asking, "Should we cut back on our print reference collections? Nobody seems to be using them," "Should we still staff the desk all the time the library is open?" and "What kind of sign should we put on the desk when nobody is there?" Clearly, things are not looking good for traditional library reference services.

DOING REFERENCE ON THE WEB

The irony in all this is that at a time when our traditional reference services are languishing from want of use, many people need exactly the kind of personal assistance we have always offered in finding what they are looking for on the Web. I'm sure each of us could verify this from the frustrations we've all endured trying to find something on the Internet ourselves. But there is now more formal evidence as well. According to the NDP Group New Media Search Satisfaction Survey in spring 2000, fully 18.6 percent of a random sample of 3,300 web users reported having difficulty finding what they were looking for "most of the time" or "all the time." Another study, called "Twelve Minutes to Search Rage" by WebTop, found that 71 percent of searchers reported getting frustrated looking for information on the Internet; the study suggested that if they had not found what they were looking for within about twelve minutes, they would be well advised to "consider some more traditional alternatives . . . for example, an information professional."

However, perhaps the best evidence that people need personalized assistance on the Internet was the swarm of companies that arose to offer personalized commercial reference services on the Web during the dot.com craze in the late 1990s. One of the best known of these commercial services was WebHelp. The service was free, and to use it all you had to do was go to their website and type in a question. In a minute or so, one of their WebWizards, as they were called, would meet you online. The two of you could converse back and forth using web chat, and the WebWizard would help you with your search and could "push" you web pages that might help answer your question, or they could take control of your browser and "escort" you around the Web to help you look for the information you needed. The WebHelp service was very popular: within seventeen weeks of opening in November 1998, it had grown to one of the top 500 most heavily trafficked sites on the Web, as measured by Nielsen and Media Metrix, and at one time it was purported to be handling more than 6,000 questions per hour using a staff of over 900 WebWizards, most of whom operated out of call centers in India. Now, just so there will be no doubt about what role WebHelp was trying to fill online, Kerry Adler, the CEO, called his WebWizards "the librarians of cyberspace," and suggested that if early growth continued unabated, he would be getting enough questions to employ over 20,000 WebWizards by the end of his first year in business. What Adler did not say, of course, is that his "librarians of cyberspace" did not require an M.L.S. degree or the years of training most of us have gone through, nor were their salaries comparable to what most of us receive, nor did they have the advantage of the tremendous print collections and other resources that libraries have built up over the years.

Unfortunately (or not), Adler never did get to hire those 20,000 WebWizards. For, not too long after he made those grandiose predictions, it became apparent that the advertising revenue he and many other commercial reference services had counted on as a potential bonanza was hardly going to be enough to pay the bills, much less deliver the kind of profits they had been expecting. When advertising didn't work out, some firms, like WebHelp, first tried charging customers for using the service, and when that failed to attract much interest, they changed their business plan altogether and focused on selling their software and services to corporations. Others, like Ask Jeeves, slashed their staff and operating expenses and hoped to make it through on much less revenue. Still others, like ExpertNet, AllExperts, Keen, and Inforocket, were absorbed and consolidated into other services. Many simply got caught up in the dot.com bust, and their services and websites have just dried up and blown away, never to be heard from again. No matter what their fate, however, it was quickly becoming clear that libraries had little to fear from commercial pretenders like Adler who had once threatened to take our place on the Web. This did not mean, of course, that libraries could just blithely ignore the experience of the commercial reference services, for while these services may have been financial failures, they were clearly a popular success. And the fact that a service like Ask Jeeves was still handling over 4 million questions per day even as it was slashing its staff by 50 percent clearly demonstrates that there is a great need for reference services on the Internet, if there were just some way to pay for them.

LIBRARY EFFORTS

To their credit, libraries did not just stand idly by as demand for traditional reference services waned and more and more of their patrons switched to the Web.

Many of these early efforts focused on making content accessible online, as libraries built websites, developed web interfaces for their online catalogs, and provided remote access to many of their subscription databases.

Reference services developed more slowly. E-mail services were the first to appear because they cost little or nothing to start up, could usually be easily handled by existing staff, and required no special technology for either the librarian or the patron. All you needed to do was post an e-mail link on your website, call it "Ask a Librarian" or something similar, and you were ready to launch into online reference.

Because they were so easy to set up, e-mail reference services proliferated on the Web in the mid-1990s, and today there are few libraries that do not offer at least this minimal level of reference service on their websites. In fact, just to show you how widely distributed e-mail reference has become, if you search on the phrase "Ask a Librarian" in Google, you will come up with over 193,000 sites that use that phrase alone, and this doesn't count the hundreds of libraries that have chosen to call their services something else, like Ask Us, Ask a Question, or even Ask Marian (from the Longmont, Colorado, Library) or any of the dozens of other names currently in use.

E-mail also permitted libraries to begin to experiment with new ways of handling reference questions for the first time. The most important of these was the development of collaborative reference services. There are potentially some great advantages in collaborative reference services, where libraries work with one another to find the answers to questions: questions can be routed to the library with the best resources or expertise to answer them; questions coming into a library that is closed can be routed to another that is open; and so on. The problem with collaboration between traditional reference services was that they were offered from a reference desk, and a librarian normally had to be physically present at that desk in order to answer questions—which made sharing questions between libraries well nigh impossible. But when the reference desk became an e-mail box online, and questions were just little electronic messages, suddenly it no longer made any difference where the librarians were located, and questions could easily be routed among a group of librarians or institutions according to subject matter, turnaround time, age level, and a number of other factors. As a result, very early on, you began to see the development of a variety of collaborative reference models. The Internet Public Library (IPL: www.ipl.org) was one of the first. The IPL takes questions from anybody online regardless of where they are, and works with a group of library school students and volunteer librarians from all over the world to help answer the hundreds of questions it receives on its website. Another well-known example is the Virtual Reference Desk project (www.vrp.org) of the Information Institute of Syracuse. It helps coordinate question-answering among dozens of "Ask-a" services (such as Ask Dr. Math, Ask a Geologist, Ask Shamu, and others) by routing questions that may be outside the scope of one service to a more appropriate source, and by working with a group of volunteer librarians to help answer the overflow, along with those questions that may not fit neatly anywhere. But the granddaddy of all the shared reference services online is the Collaborative Digital Reference Service (CDRS), pioneered by the Library of Congress and more than 200 libraries from around the world. At present this is a library-to-library service. Librarians who find they cannot answer a question with their own resources can submit their question to the CDRS Network, which automatically routes the question to the most appropriate library on the network. CDRS is also experimenting with building a knowledge base of the questions and answers it creates, in the hope that patrons may someday be able to find many of their answers among questions that have already been asked—and thus avoid talking with a librarian altogether—unless, of course, they want to.

E-mail reference services were a quick and easy way for libraries to move their reference services to the Web. The technology also allowed us to begin to experiment with collaborative reference and a number of other innovations never possible before. But e-mail reference also posed some serious problems for both the librarian and the patron. The first—and perhaps greatest—of these was speed, or rather the lack of it. There is nothing inherently slow about e-mail. If you have librarians dedicated to watching the e-mail box, they can pick up e-mail questions and answer them within minutes, just as we would if that question were asked at the reference desk. The problem is that there are few libraries that can dedicate staff to handling e-mail alone, so in practice most libraries have offered a 24–48-hour turnaround. Some, like the IPL, only promise three days, and others won't even commit to that. Now, if you're a patron doing a search in the library catalog, and you're having trouble trying to remember an author's name, or you're a student with a paper due the next day who's just looking for a few good articles, or you are almost anyone else with a pressing question (and which of our questions are not pressing, anyway?), then that 24–48-hour turnaround is going to seem like a very long time indeed—particularly when search engines will often turn up some reasonable results in a matter of a few seconds—and many patrons will be tempted to look elsewhere for an answer.

But speed is not the only problem. When you are working with a patron online, you'd like the process to be as natural and realistic as possible. It should be the next best thing to being there. Ideally, the experience should resemble sitting down beside the patron at a workstation. The two of you should be able to see each other and talk back and forth. You should be able to take control of the browser and show the patron relevant websites, or how to do a search. You should be able to see and help correct patrons' search strategies and help get them back on track if things don't turn out the way you expected. There is no technology presently on the market that will allow you to do all of these things, although some are approaching it. But e-mail doesn't even come close. At best it is like sitting down and writing notes to the patron . . . and you can't even be sure when the responses will come back. There is very little that is natural or interactive about it. And since the reference transaction often requires a fair amount of conversation with the patron, first to find out what they really want, then to find out what they've done so far, then to find out if what you located is helpful, and so on, it is easy to see why so many librarians and patrons alike have found that e-mail reference can be a frustrating and time-consuming experience.

There is one other serious disadvantage to e-mail reference. The librarian ends up doing much of the work. At the regular reference desk, the librarian and the patron often work together to find the information the patron is looking for. Often the librarian would take the patron to the catalog or the most appropriate database and show them how to search for the topic, and then the librarian would go off to check additional sources or help other patrons. Meanwhile, the patron has shouldered much of the burden of finding the answer, under professional direction, of course. With e-mail reference, the patron is not there to help with the work, so librarians typically end up answering the question from start to finish. Add to that the fact you also have to write the answer up in some sort of intelligible format, and a simple question that might have taken a few minutes' time to handle at the regular reference desk can take several times that long when answered in e-mail.

To further complicate matters, most library e-mail reference services have attracted very little traffic. Libraries set them up and made elaborate contingency plans and backup arrangements to handle the horde of questions they were sure would be coming. But except for a few very large and well-known institutions, like the Library of Congress, the public has made very little use of e-mail reference services. Although it should be much easier for a patron to ask a question online than it is to travel to the library, few libraries report receiving more than a few questions per day via e-mail, a tiny fraction of what they are getting at the regular reference desk. And remember that in most cases, the numbers of questions being asked at the desk are already well down from their historical norms. This is not a very auspicious beginning for a service that many had hoped would help establish libraries' unique value on the Web. There is probably a variety of reasons why electronic reference services don't seem to have taken off as quickly as we had hoped. We will consider those reasons in some detail later. But certainly one of the contributing factors with e-mail reference service is the frustrations of the format itself. After all, it is pretty hard to attract the attention of a public that is used to fast and increasingly accurate search engines, real-time chat, and live interactive services when all you have to offer is e-mail with a 24-hour turnaround, if you are lucky.

I don't mean to imply here that e-mail reference does not have its place. Clearly it does. It can be a very effective tool for following up with a patron when a question cannot be answered fully live and in real time. It works very well for routing questions in collaborative systems like the CDRS. It offers a degree of anonymity for those who may be afraid to ask certain kinds of questions in person, and it probably works just fine for questions that don't have any time constraints. But for the rest of us who do have time constraints, or who are struggling to search a library catalog or figure out what database we should be looking in, e-mail reference is a very poor substitute for the kind of service we had been able to expect from a real librarian behind a real reference desk. Clearly another solution was needed, and libraries began to look for other, more interactive technologies that might better help move reference services online.

INTERACTIVE REFERENCE SERVICES

The earliest experiments with interactive reference technologies involved MOOs, or *m*ultiuser *o*bject-*o*riented environments. These were text-based "virtual reality" programs that were originally designed to be used with fantasy role-playing games like Dungeons and Dragons. The Internet Public Library tried applying this "technology" for reference purposes on an experimental basis starting in 1995 and continuing on and off through February 2000. (You can see a description of the project and a link to the final report at http://www.ipl.org/moo/.)

In concept, a MOO worked like a big chat room with a virtual floor plan. People could enter and move about the MOO and chat with one another by typing commands. Typing "North," for example, might move you from the virtual foyer to the virtual reference room, and typing "@say I've got a question" would tell the librarian—and anyone else who happened to be in the room—that you had a question. Like chat rooms, any number of parties could enter and start holding conversations with one another and with the librarians in the room all at the same time.

MOOs might have been wonderful for fantasy games, but they proved to be quite cumbersome for reference purposes. On the plus side, the technology did allow librarians and patrons to talk and interact with each other live and in real time, and it could be accessed by almost anyone regardless of the speed of their Internet connection or what type of computer or operating system they were using. However, in practice it was difficult for both librarians and patrons to learn and remember all the arcane text commands necessary to interact in the MOO (most of which were unnecessary for reference purposes anyway). Conversations were often jumbled and confusing because everybody in the room could be talking at the same time (this is a problem in any chat room), and interaction was limited to chat alone; a librarian had no way to show the patron a web page, for example; all they could do is describe it. MOOs were an interesting early attempt to add some interactivity to the Web, but they were never broadly adopted for reference purposes, and the technology itself quickly became antiquated as gamers and the rest of us discovered new and better ways to work together on the Web.

One of those new and better ways appeared to be desktop videoconferencing. If the MOO represented the most rudimentary form of interactivity on the Web, desktop videoconferencing lies all the way at the other end of the spectrum. Here both the librarian and the patron have cameras and microphones mounted on their computers so they can see and talk with each other during the reference session, and these are normally coupled with software that allows both parties to share applications, white boards, and a variety of other online collaborative tools. In 1997 the University of California at Irvine (UCI) tried an experimental program using desktop videoconferencing to provide remote reference services between its Science Library and the Medical Center Library located a few miles away. Both the librarian's computer and the remote reference computer were equipped with cameras and microphones and videoconferencing software, and both had high-speed T1 connections to the Internet. (See figure 1-4 for a screenshot of the UCI interface.) In those days, desktop videoconferencing technology was still a little clunky (many would say it still is), but by and large, librarians and patrons at UCI found they were able to work together on catalog and Medline searches, look at web pages together, and chat back and forth with one another . . . all while they checked out the expressions on each others' faces.

It may be that sometime in the future, desktop videoconferencing—or something very much like it—will become the primary technology for online reference (although the thought of working in front of a camera bothers more than a few librarians). When videoconferencing is working well over good high-speed network connections, it truly can be the next best thing to being there. The problem right now is that both the librarian's and the patron's computers must be equipped with all the necessary hardware and software . . . and both computers must be carefully tested and configured to work together in advance . . . and both need to have fairly high-speed connections to the Internet in order to handle all of the audio, video, and other data passing between them without choking up. What this means is that, at present, the only practical application of desktop videoconferencing technology is to provide remote reference service between already established sites, as in the UCI project. But it is virtually impossible to use it—or any technology that requires special hardware

FIGURE 1-4 Desktop videoconferencing at the University of California at Irvine

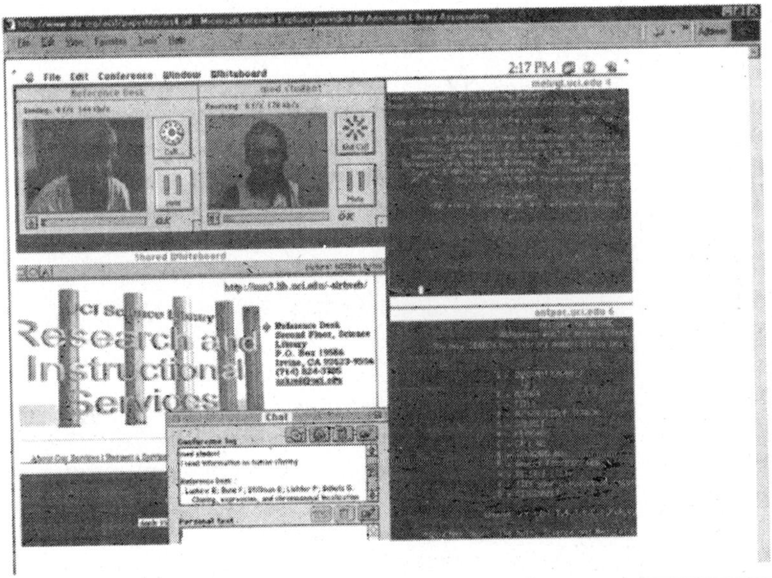

configurations, large software downloads, and high-speed connections—to serve the average patron out on the Internet who just happens to stumble across your library's website from their home or office computer.

Apart from these initial experiments with MOOs and desktop videoconferencing, much of the early development work with virtual reference focused on Internet chat software. At their most basic, chat programs are very simple applications that allow a librarian and a patron to "chat" with each other in real time by typing text messages back and forth—just as you might in a standard chat room. The only difference is that most library chat software is designed for one-on-one interactions between a librarian and a patron, so you are not forced to share your questions with a whole room full of people as you were in those early MOOs, or in chat rooms on AOL, for that matter. Chat software is also easy to use; all you have to do is type. There are no arcane commands to learn, and you don't need to know how to move around in some virtual space, as you did in a MOO. And unlike desktop videoconferencing, chat can be used on almost any computer and on almost any connection. It does not require any special hardware, software, or configuration, and it runs just fine over a standard dial-up Internet connection. Finally, it is cheap. Most chat software is either available for free or at very low cost. In fact, many of the earliest chat software used in libraries were homegrown applications created by student programmers, and some of these are still in use. The earliest documented use of chat software for reference service was at the State University of New York at Morrisville in 1997 using a homegrown program created by Bill Drew. The service is still up and running and you can visit it today at http://library.morrisville.edu, although they have since switched to AOL's Instant Messenger for their chat service. Other early entrants also used locally developed software, including Temple University's Temple TalkNow (http://www.library.temple.edu/ref/ask_us.htm), which started operating in 1998, and the University of North Texas Library's Online Reference Help Desk (http://www.library.unt.edu/chatroom/default.htm), which began operating in May 1999. Both of these services are still in operation using versions of the original software as of this writing.

Chat reference software has continued to evolve from these early efforts. Perhaps the most important developments were the introduction of low-cost commercial chat applications such as HumanClick and the various instant messaging programs available for free from AOL, Microsoft, Yahoo, and others. These programs work much like the early chat software—in that their primary function is to allow people to communicate online by typing text messages back and forth—but they have added a variety of "bells and whistles." For example, many instant messaging programs allow you to send small pictures or other files back and forth. Most will allow you to add "emoticons" or "smileys" to your chat to convey a little emotion with your messages. You can have the computer play a typing sound so the other parties to the conversation know you are writing a message. Many programs now allow you to "talk" online using VoIP (voice over Internet Protocol), although the voice quality is very poor on most connections. And some even allow you to see a picture of the other person if they happen to have a web cam. Some of these features had been available in high-end desktop videoconferencing or web contact center software. The difference was that now they could be had for nothing just by downloading one of the commercial instant messaging programs.

Chat software made it relatively easy and inexpensive for libraries to set up interactive online reference services for the first time, and it was not long before chat reference services were showing up on library websites all over the world. Today these chat programs remain one of the most popular methods of doing virtual reference, and they are certainly still the quickest and cheapest way for a library to set up shop on the Web. Exact numbers are impossible to come by, but approximately 30 percent of the libraries listed on the two virtual reference registries (Stephen Francoeur's Teaching Librarian site at http://pages.prodigy.net/tabo1/digref.htm and Gerry McKiernan's LiveRef at http://www.public.iastate.edu/~CYBERSTACKS/LiveRef.htm) used some form of chat or instant messaging software as of January 2002. There are some chat adherents who feel strongly that basic chat software is all you really need to do virtual reference, and that the more sophisticated and elaborate virtual reference software applications that are now available are just a waste of money.

However, chat software also has its problems. In the first place, it was designed for, well, chat—which is to say, social conversations between friends. The problem is that online reference is much more than a conversation among friends. The primary purpose of online reference, or any reference service for that matter, is to assist patrons in finding the information they need. This often requires more than just talking. Ideally, you'd like to be able to share web pages with a patron, or escort them through one of your library's online databases, or help them to develop or refine a search strategy, or to scan and send an image from your print collection. But chat software supports none of these functions, or supports them only in the most rudimentary fashion.

Secondly, chat software was designed for one-on-one conversations between individuals, not for handling large volumes of questions on heavily trafficked library reference services. As long as your library is only getting a few questions a day and those questions normally come in one at a time, there is no problem. But as your traffic increases, and you have multiple patrons wanting service at the same time, and multiple librarians have logged on to handle the demand, you need some way of queuing patrons and routing them to the next available librarian. There is no provision for queuing and routing in basic chat or instant messaging software, however.

Next there is the problem of downloading the software. All of the instant messaging programs currently in use require that the patron download and set up "client" software on their computer before they can chat with anybody. Software downloads have been the kiss of death for many applications because people tend to be a little cautious about downloading some unknown program to their computer, unless it's an MP3 player. And even if you can convince them to do it, it is often difficult to get the software to set up and operate the way it is supposed to on all the different machines people are using out there. The download issue is less of a problem with instant messaging software because many people have already downloaded it to talk with their friends, and even if they haven't, most instant messaging software comes from very well-known (and hence less scary) sources like AOL, Microsoft, Yahoo, etc. So it's not as if the library is asking patrons to download some obscure plug-in just so they can chat with a librarian. Nevertheless, each of the instant messaging services uses its own proprietary interface, none of which talk with one another. So if a library decides to use the AOL program, and the patron has Microsoft or Yahoo instant messaging, the patron has to download a free AOL Instant Messenger program before they can ask a question.

Finally, there are issues of privacy and ownership of the reference transcripts with instant messaging software. All of those instant messages go through the servers of the host network, and are subject to the terms of use and theoretically, at least, to the inspection of AOL, MSN, and other providers. This raises more than a few concerns about patron privacy and what use others might make of information shared in reference sessions. Of course, these concerns don't seem to deter millions of people from exchanging hundreds of millions of instant messages with each other every day (one source reports that AOL alone is handling an average of over 805 million messages per day), but libraries have always had a special concern for patron privacy, and commercial instant messaging programs do introduce a third party to the transaction, a party that may not always share the same concerns and values as we do.

So while inexpensive chat software helped introduce many libraries to the joys of virtual reference service, its limitations soon had many of them looking for a more sophisticated solution that is better tailored for doing reference work on the Web. And they found it in web contact center software.

Web contact center software—also sometimes called "web collaboration software," or "live interaction software"—was originally developed for live customer service on e-commerce sites like L.L.Bean and Lands End. Like chat software, web contact center applications allow customers and customer service reps or librarians and patrons to "talk" with each other on the Web, but they also do much more. Even the simplest of these applications usually allows a librarian to share web pages with a patron, and the more advanced applications include a variety of interactive tools. The most sophisticated applications allow librarians to actually take control of a patron's browser and escort them around the Web; the librarian and patron can share text in search boxes and web forms so they can develop search strategies together. Some software allows librarians and patrons to work together in library subscription databases, and a number offer the ability to share slideshows, screenshots, files, scanned images, and a rich variety of other content with patrons. The list continues to grow as these applications develop.

Moreover, because web contact center software was designed for handling large numbers of questions on heavily trafficked websites, most of this software includes at lease some queuing and routing functions, as well as features like scripted messages, bookmarks, internal knowledge bases, the ability to work with more than one patron at the same time, and various other features designed to make it easier for customer service representatives or librarians to handle large numbers of questions online. Finally, e-commerce companies wanted to make it as easy as possible for customers to reach them online; so—unlike instant messaging services—most web contact center applications require no software downloads on the patron's side, and most will also work with a wide variety of computers, connections, and operating systems.

With the development of web contact center software, libraries finally seemed to have found the tools they needed to develop the first true production-quality virtual reference services on the Web. And some libraries were quick to try it out. The University of Calgary experimented with a web contact center application called NetEffect in the spring of 1998, and Cornell University started a pilot project with LivePerson—a comparatively inexpensive application—in the fall of 1998.

However, web contact center software still remained well out of reach of the average library's budget, and even if a library could afford it, the software had a reputation for being difficult to install and maintain. Moreover, even though the software worked better than anything else that had been tried up to that point, a substantial amount of work still had to be done to adapt it for reference purposes—including modifying it for co-browsing online databases, adding IP authentication, and a variety of other features. Then there was the issue of training the reference staff—most of whom had never typed a line of chat in their lives. In order to address these problems, a number of companies and library consortia—

including LSSI, the Metropolitan Cooperative Library System, and others—developed specially adapted versions of web contact center software that were designed and priced to accommodate the library market. And with that, virtual reference service in libraries really took off.

I remember back in the early days—spring of 1999—I could keep track of all the existing virtual library projects with the fingers on one hand. But over the past few years, the growth has been so rapid, and there are so many different libraries using so many different software packages, that it is no longer possible to come up with an exact count of all the libraries doing reference online. Stephen Francoeur and Gerry McKiernan both try to maintain registries of virtual reference services. Francoeur's Teaching Librarian website listed about 200 services as of January 2002, and McKiernan's LiveRef site listed about 100 services as of the same date. But both listings lag behind the real numbers by a fairly significant amount. I know that LSSI alone provided virtual reference services to more than 300 libraries as of early 2002, and if you add these to the numbers listed on the two registries, my guess is that anywhere between 500 and 600 libraries are now offering some sort of live reference service on the Web, with about 70 percent of them now using web contact center software of one brand or another, and that number is growing at an amazing pace.

So there you have it: a brief history of library reference services on the Web. I wish I could conclude this chapter by telling you that libraries had indeed succeeded in rejoining our patrons on the Web and attracted thousands of new users who had never graced our doors before. I wish I could say that we had proven that the only ones good enough, smart enough, and experienced enough to call themselves the "librarians of cyberspace" were real librarians, like you and I, who had spent some time behind the desk and who knew that there was much more to reference than just pushing web pages at people. I wish I could show you that libraries had filled the void left by the demise of the dot.com reference services and that our sites were just as heavily trafficked as the WebHelps and Ask Jeeves on the Net who had once pretended to take our place. And I wish I could tell you that those of us who have gone before you had finally figured it all out, and there was a simple recipe I could give you that would guarantee a successful reference service on the Web. But in truth, I can do none of these things.

Virtual reference services are only in their infancy on the Web. Although there are hundreds of us now, none of us have been around all that long. There are not really any stunning successes to point to yet, nor, thankfully, any abject failures. All virtual reference projects are pilot projects. None of us have yet got it figured out.

Though they are still young, web-based reference services are already facing major challenges that could threaten the future of these services. Fundamental questions arise like: Do people really need reference services on the Web? If we build them, will they come? And if they do come, how will we handle them? Make no mistake about it, resolving these issues will not be easy, and developing successful reference services on the Web will likely require a very careful rethinking of the entire reference process, both on the Web and at the desk. There are as yet no answers to these questions, but many of us are struggling to find them.

So the purpose of this book is not so much to instruct you in the ways of virtual reference, but rather to invite you into this world. To introduce you to the various approaches libraries are taking in the design and operation of these systems. To point out known problems and show you some of the solutions people are working on. To discuss the various methods libraries are experimenting with to market their services on the Web; those that have been successful, and those that have not. And finally, to look ahead a little and speculate on where all of this may lead us if we are successful in moving our reference services to the Web. The hope is that those of you starting such services now will be able to benefit from the trials and tribulations of those of us who have gone before you, and that together we may find answers to the major issues facing us, and help libraries rejoin our patrons on the Web.

NOTES

1. A total of 301 million searches per Search Engine Watch, at www.searchenginewatch.com (accessed 10 January 2002); 309.6 million searches per National Center for Education Statistics data for 1996 academic libraries and 1997 public libraries. (The latter figure was the most recent data available from the NCES at the time of this writing; current figures may actually be lower.)
2. See http://fisher.lib.virginia.edu/arl/index.html, cyberatlas.internet.com, and http://www.nielsen-netratings.com.

CHAPTER TWO

Getting Started

Designing Virtual Reference Systems

Start talking about designing virtual reference systems, and many people immediately begin to conjure up images of a Herculean task that is sure to require dozens of staff, all kinds of committees, tens of thousands of dollars, and many months to complete. That's a pretty fair description of what it has taken to get some of the major virtual reference projects up and running. On the other hand, you have examples like Colorado Community College, which managed to implement a full-scale 24-hour a day virtual reference service for a few thousand dollars and went live in less than 24 hours with nary a committee involved. Virtual reference is not rocket science. There is nothing inherently expensive or complex about it. It can be, and has been, undertaken by libraries of all types and sizes. The difficulty and cost of the project depend on how you want to use the technology, and how many libraries and staff you want to include in the project. So before you rush out and start setting up software selection committees and jump into writing those grant applications, it is a good idea to sit down and think about how you want to start using virtual reference in your library—for it is that decision which will govern all the other elements of your system design, from the type of software you'll need to the type of people you will need to staff it.

WHAT DO YOU WANT TO DO WITH IT?

Most of us begin to explore virtual reference with one idea in mind—we'd like to provide our patrons with reference services over the Web—just as we have done from behind our reference desks. However, while a full-scale, around-the-clock web reference service may be the highest use of virtual reference technology, designing and implementing such a service is no easy task, and doing it right can require a fairly significant commitment of staff and resources, as you'll discover reading through this chapter.

Reference is only one of the many uses of this new technology. Virtual reference software allows library staff and patrons to communicate and interact with one another in real time over the Web. The same technology that allows you to answer a reference question live on the Web can also be put to use in a number of other library applications, most of which require much less staff and resources than a full-scale virtual reference service. So, if you'd like to do virtual reference but find it might be a bit out of your reach at the moment, you may want to consider some of these other uses libraries have found for the technology.

Online Office Hours

Some libraries are using the software to offer virtual office hours with a librarian. This approach is used in academic libraries where students and faculty are encouraged to make an online appointment with the librarian and both parties can then explore online resources together. Conversation can be handled over the phone or with chat, and the software can be used for collaboration and co-browsing. This service simply duplicates online something many of us already do in person, except the patron can now work with the librarian without having to travel to the library . . . and the librarian only logs on and uses the software when they have an appointment scheduled. They do not have to be tied to the computer for hours every day as is often the case when you are running an online reference service.

Online Bibliographic Instruction

Some virtual reference applications have an online meeting facility that libraries have been using to offer "classroom style" bibliographic instruction over the Web. So now, instead of—or more typically, in addition to—going over to Professor Smith's Psychology 101 class and letting students know about all of the databases and other resources you have available to help them get started on their papers, you can invite them to log on to your online classroom at an appointed time, and you can give them a live tour of many of your electronic resources on the Web. Here again, this type of session is much easier to work into your schedule than a full-scale virtual reference service, and it offers some decided advantages to the students as well . . . particularly if they are distance education students who may be nowhere near the campus. Of course, you don't need to keep the technology all to yourself either; it might earn you some brownie points to offer it to other faculty for use in their online classes too.

Online Programming

Software that can be used to hold online classes can also be used to handle all sorts of online programming. If you were in a public library, you might invite experts to hold online programs on all kinds of topics . . . just as you do in your library meeting rooms. This approach would also work well for academic libraries. You could schedule an online lecture series on interesting faculty projects or offer online versions of selected library programs and events. There are also internal applications, because the same technology could be used to provide online training sessions—particularly on web-related subjects—for your own staff.

Library-to-Library Reference Services

A number of libraries are looking at virtual reference software as a way to enable staff at general reference desks to access specialized services at subject-specialty or second-level reference services. For example, a large library system might use virtual reference software to connect branch libraries directly with staff in a reference subject specialty center. Using this model, if a patron in one of the branches has a business question that cannot be answered with the local collection, the branch librarian can simply click on the virtual reference link on a computer at the reference desk, and put the patron in direct contact with expert staff at the subject specialty center.

Some library vendors and database producers are also looking at this model as a way of delivering specialized subscription-based reference services over the Web. For example, if your library does not have its own business subject specialty service, in the future you may be able to subscribe to a service offered by the James J. Hill Reference Library in St. Paul, Minnesota. LSSI is offering libraries Spanish and Chinese language reference services delivered with virtual reference technology. Other vendors are looking at using the same model to offer specialized legal and health information services.

If you don't see anything that interests you here, new applications are being developed all the time. Virtual reference has many applications worth exploring. Just make sure you have a pretty good idea of how you are going to use it before you get started, since the decisions you make at this point will govern the way you design your system, and the software, staffing, and other resources you need to implement it.

HOW ARE YOU GOING TO DO IT?

Once you've figured out what you want to do with virtual reference technology, it's time to sit down and give some serious thought to how you are going to do it, and with whom you are going to work. The technology allows a lot of flexibility in the design of virtual reference services. You can do it all yourself, you can have somebody do everything for you, or you can work with others, either purchasing services from commercial reference providers or working with a consortium to share services among yourselves. Let's consider each of these options separately.

Doing It Yourself

One option is to do it all yourself. You design the system according to your own specifications, and nobody else's. You select the software that best fits the way you want to use your system, and you purchase and operate it on your own. You choose what databases and resources you want to use. You establish your own service policies and procedures. You set the quality standards. And most importantly, you find the staff you are going to need to operate the service all the hours it is to be open . . . including somebody to cover those lonely graveyard shifts if you're hoping to run a 24-hour service.

The do-it-yourself model has several great advantages over the collaborative reference services that some libraries are trying. First off, it is what we are used to. While cataloging, interlibrary lending (ILL), and some other important library functions have long been cooperative ventures, reference has traditionally been a service each library has done pretty much on its own. We are not accustomed to having our reference work scrutinized by others, nor are we in the habit of modifying our service policies and procedures to fit the needs of others. Many of us would just as soon see it stay that way. Moreover, those libraries that have worked to develop truly world-class reference services might want to think long and hard before they turn over responsibility for serving their patrons to reference staff from other institutions who may not share the same values—even if it is only for a few hours.

On the other hand, as we've said before, developing and operating a great virtual reference service is no easy task. To set up a truly full-featured system can cost tens of thousands of dollars, and staffing it—even during regular business hours—can require more time than can easily be carved out of the schedules of your existing reference librarians. Just see how far you get when you ask for volunteers to stay up until 3 a.m. in the morning. However, if you have the money and the staff, doing it yourself clearly gives you the greatest control over your service, and for some libraries, nothing less will do.

Buying It from Others

If doing it all yourself sounds like a bit more than your library can handle at the moment, then you might want to consider purchasing virtual reference services from others. A number of vendors and libraries have started offering complete subscription virtual reference services in the past year or so which libraries can purchase just as they do electronic databases—the only difference is that the librarians are included. These services are typically sold by the question—often in bundles of questions—and usually feature everything you need to start a virtual reference service on your library website, including both software and reference staff, plus all of the customization necessary to make it look and feel like your own. These turnkey services are available from commercial vendors like LSSI, as well as from a few virtual reference consortia like Clevenet, which is offering its KnowItNow service to other libraries in Ohio. Eglobal Library is even selling a complete turnkey library service, which includes both its electronic content and a fully staffed virtual reference service, and other database vendors are considering similar products as of this writing.

Turnkey services are perfect for libraries that do not have adequate staff to run a service on their own, or for those that want to get a service up and running quickly, or, in the case of the Eglobal Library product, for institutions that may not have a library at all.

If a complete turnkey reference service was not exactly what you had in mind, you may want to consider outsourcing your after-hours service.

This is a very common practice with libraries offering 24/7 services, since most libraries have found it next to impossible to get their own reference staff to work during the wee hours of the morning. A number of libraries are also using outsourced staff to help cover peak periods (sometimes called "overflow coverage"), which can make a lot of sense when you just need another librarian to help handle the questions for an hour or so, or to help deal with the blitz of traffic you can get after the local newspaper runs an article on your service.

After-hours and overflow services are typically sold in bundles of questions, just like turnkey services (although some vendors are beginning to experiment with full-time equivalent [FTE] and other population-based models), but the library determines the schedule it wants the outside service to cover.

Whether you're buying a full turnkey system or just need coverage during after-hours, outsourcing virtual reference services clearly has some advantages. It allows you to purchase services that might be difficult to develop yourself. It allows you to get up and running quickly, since the outsourced staff are already trained and ready to go. In many cases, the staff from the outsourced service may be more experienced and hence better able to offer virtual reference services than your own people. But there are also some disadvantages to outsourced services. Some reference is clearly local; staff from a reference call center a thousand miles away may not be able to answer questions that require some knowledge of your town or campus. This problem can be mitigated to some extent by making sure that the remote staff are tightly integrated with your own reference department and that there are good referral procedures in place for questions that cannot be answered effectively by the remote staff. Another problem is that if you outsource your virtual reference services entirely, it means your staff does not get the opportunity to develop their own skills and you are dependent on others for those services. Of course, that sort of arrangement is hardly new to the library profession, and most of us have been outsourcing large amounts of our cataloging services to the Library of Congress and the OCLC for a long time. Finally, you are turning over control of part of your reference services to someone else that may not share the same standards for quality and customer service that you do. However, one advantage of paying for reference services is that you can stipulate the standards the vendor must adhere to, and you do have recourse if they do not deliver—something that is not always possible with the consortial cooperative reference services we'll look at next.

Collaborating with Others

In collaborative reference services, a group of libraries join together to provide virtual reference services as a group. Collaborative reference services are still very new, and in many respects, they have only become possible with the development of virtual reference software that allows libraries to share staffing of a "virtual reference desk" over the Internet. In a typical collaborative reference service, libraries normally share a single installation of the software, and staff a single "virtual reference desk" that can be accessed from all participating libraries. Librarians from all participating libraries take turns staffing the virtual desk a few hours each week—and during their shifts, they answer questions coming in from all of the member libraries. Librarians working in collaborative services usually train together and work with a common set of policies and procedures to ensure consistency in the level of service patrons can expect. A number of collaborative projects have purchased a core set of reference resources together, to ensure that all patrons would have access to a "core" reference collection, no matter what library they were coming from. Some libraries are also beginning to work on shared marketing plans for their services. There are numerous variations on this theme, and more are being developed all the time as libraries continue to experiment with this new way of doing reference.

Most collaborative reference services have been built upon preexisting consortia. Among them are the KnowItNow project (http://www.cpl.org/vrd/learnmore.html), a group of about 30 libraries in the Cleveland, Ohio, area that were built inside the Clevenet consortium; the QandANJ project (http://www.qandanj.org), which developed out of the South Jersey Regional Library Cooperative but has now grown to include dozens of libraries of all types throughout the state of New Jersey; and the Ready for Reference project (http://www.alliancelibrarysystem.com/projects/readyref/index.html), involving eight academic libraries in central Illinois which are all members of the Alliance Library System. These local consortia have generally worked pretty well; in fact, the busiest and most heavily used virtual reference services currently in operation are all based on local consortia.

Some libraries are also beginning to experiment with "ad hoc" consortia, developed specifically for offering virtual reference services. These differ from more traditional consortia because the libraries involved usually have had little or nothing to do with each other before they get together to provide reference services, so they lack the shared infrastructure and relationships found in collaborative services built on existing consortia. Often these ad hoc collaboratives are formed to share the cost of the software, such as the 24/7 Reference service, which started as a local consortium for libraries in southern California but now makes its virtual reference software available to any library that wants to "buy in." Libraries are also looking at ad hoc consortia as a way of sharing reference services across time zones. The commonly discussed arrangement is to set up a 24-hour reference service staffed by libraries in the United States, Australia, and Europe. However, these "follow-the-sun" collaboratives have been much easier to describe than they are to create. As of this writing, the first one involving public libraries in Brisbane, Australia, Somerset, U.K., and Richland County, South Carolina, was just getting under way. However, there are a number of academic collaboratives involving libraries in the United States, Australia, Canada, Spain, and the United Kingdom that are in the active planning stages.

Collaborative services offer several advantages. First, they help keep the costs down. When ten or twenty libraries are sharing one virtual reference system, the cost per participating library is much less than if any one of the members tried to purchase the same system on its own. This also applies to marketing, advertising, and other expensive services that would be well beyond the reach of any single library purchasing on its own. Secondly, collaborative services help keep the traffic up. Ask any veteran on a virtual reference desk and they will tell you that these systems are often slow to be discovered, and there are few things more damaging to morale than having a bunch of well-trained and enthusiastic librarians sitting in front of computers waiting for someone to call. Collaborative services help address this problem by expanding the potential "market" for the service to the patrons of all member libraries, greatly minimizing the chances that librarians will be sitting for hours with nothing to do.

But the most important benefit of collaborative reference services is shared staffing. In a typical collaborative, each member library is responsible for covering the virtual reference desk for a certain number of hours per week, depending on the number of libraries involved and the schedule they want to operate. For example, if you wanted to operate the service from 9 a.m. to 9 p.m., 7 days per week, and you wanted to staff the desk with two librarians at all times the service was open, your total staffing requirement would be 168 hours per week (12 hours × 7 days × 2 librarians). Now, if you had 10 libraries participating in a collaborative reference service, and each could contribute 3 librarians, each librarian would be required to staff the virtual desk only 5.6 hours per week, yet all 10 libraries would be able to offer a very full reference schedule. If any one of those 10 libraries tried to offer the same schedule all on their own, each of their 3 librarians would need to spend 56 hours per week on the desk . . . something that might get you into a little bit of trouble with the labor laws, to say nothing of the librarians who actually had to do it.

Of course, collaborative services also have their disadvantages. These have much in common with the potential problems you can run into with outsourced reference services as discussed previously. This is because collaborative reference services are really a form of outsourced reference services, except in this case, instead of purchasing reference services from a vendor, you are, in effect, bartering for them with other libraries in the collaborative. But no matter how you are paying for them, you are turning over some of your reference services to someone outside your institution. And whenever you turn your reference services over to someone you do not control, you have to be concerned with the quality of the service they might provide. The only difference here is that if you are not satisfied with the service delivered by a commercial vendor, you normally have some way to enforce the contract . . . including firing the vendor and refusing to pay for services delivered. In a collaborative reference service, however, your remedies may not be so clear, nor as easy to enforce. Likewise, handling questions that require local knowledge may be a problem in collaborative reference services just as it is in outsourced arrangements. It is important that there be good procedures in place for referring questions that require local knowledge and resources back to the local library. Despite these potential problem areas, collaborative services are already playing a crucial role in the development of virtual reference services, and if libraries really can learn how to share their services effectively, in the future collaborative reference may one day be as common as cooperative cataloging.

DESIGNING YOUR VIRTUAL REFERENCE SYSTEM

Once you've determined how you are going to use your virtual reference system, and you've decided whether you are going to build it and operate it entirely on your own, outsource it entirely, purchase services from a commercial reference services provider, share the work with other libraries in a consortium, or some combination of the above, you are ready to sit down and start designing a virtual reference system to meet your needs.

Designing a virtual reference service really involves answering three key questions.

1. What kind of software should I use?
2. How many and what kind of staff will I need to operate the system? Once you've got these two answered, you'll have the information you need to answer the most critical question of all:
3. How much is all of this going to cost me anyway?

Let's tackle these one at a time.

What Kind of Virtual Reference Software Should I Use?

Despite the claims of a few vendors, the perfect virtual reference software does not yet exist, and probably won't for some time to come. Ultimately, what we need is a software application that (1) makes it as easy to communicate and share information with patrons on the Web as it is when they are standing in front of the desk; (2) takes advantage of all the new collaborative opportunities and productivity features now available online; and (3) is available at a cost almost any library could afford.

There are a number of companies working to create that perfect system, and perhaps someday one of them will succeed. Until then, we are left to choose from a growing number of software packages, offering a truly bewildering array of features, in a variety of price ranges—none of which is perfectly suited to our needs.

Each of these products has its own strengths and weaknesses. Choosing the right product for your virtual reference service involves some trade-offs between a few key criteria: the feature set offered by a software package; how easy the software is for patrons to use; the level of support you can expect from the vendor; and finally, the cost of the software. Here are some suggestions for how to go about balancing these key criteria and selecting a software product that best meets your needs.

FEATURE SET

Your first and foremost consideration in selecting virtual reference software should be the feature set. Put simply, you have to make sure the software you select will support the use you want to make of it. If you intend to use your virtual reference service for online bibliographic instruction classes, the software you choose had better be able to support online meetings where there is more than one patron in a session. If you intend to use your software to help patrons inside your online databases, you'll need software that can handle database co-browsing. The list can go on and on. Collectively, the software products currently on the market offer hundreds and hundreds of features, and more are being added every day. To help you make sense of these, you will find a comprehensive list of the features available in the most commonly used virtual reference software applications as of spring 2002 in appendix A, along with detailed explanations of what they do and how they are used. Depending on the type of service you want to operate, some of these features may be truly critical, others are just optional or nice to have, and some may be worthless or even get in the way.

EASE OF USE

Once you've put your basic list of features together, you'll want to give some careful thought to just how much you want to require of the patrons who will be using your system. Unfortunately, some of the most sophisticated interactive features like audio and video come with strings attached that can make it much more difficult for patrons to access and use your service. The issue is whether you are going to require your patrons to download software to access and use your service. This has been a showstopper for many services because patrons have often proved unwilling to download special software just to ask a question, and downloads can introduce security concerns. However, this may not be as much of an issue if you are working in a corporate or campus environment where you may already be downloading software to patron computers. In addition to the download issue, you also need to consider other requirements the software may impose on the patron. Some packages only work with PCs, and not with Macs or Unix platforms, some only work with certain browser versions, and some may require very high-speed Internet connections in order to use sophisticated features like video or voice over IP. No matter what you choose, you always need to think carefully about the patron's experience on your software, for the most wonderful feature in the world is no good if your patrons refuse to use it.

SUPPORT

Another important criterion in selecting a product is support. Many of the products you will be reviewing were not designed for the library market. Many of the software companies barely know libraries exist, much less how you might use their software in reference applications. However, if you are reading this book, chances are you already know that setting up virtual reference service can be a difficult process, and you can use all the help and support you can get. So, all other things being equal, you should give some thought to how much the vendor understands the needs of libraries; and to the level of support for system design, training, marketing, and other issues that may be available from the company or from other libraries that may already be using that software.

SOFTWARE COSTS

Finally, all of us have to think about cost. It is important in doing so not to focus on the price of the software alone, but to keep the whole cost of operating your virtual reference service in mind, and the ways the functionality of the software might affect that. For example, in the long run, staff costs will be your greatest overall expense in operating a virtual reference service. So software that allows librarians to handle multiple patrons at the same time may save you thousands of dollars in staff costs, even though it may cost more initially. Also, give some thought to ways to share the cost. Today many virtual reference services are operated by library consortia, where the actual cost per participating library can be quite low.

RESEARCHING THE FIELD

Once you have selected the features which are important to you, and given some consideration to ease of use, support, and cost, make a list of the software packages you want to review. If you limit your list to companies that are working with the library marketplace or to software that libraries have already adapted for virtual reference, these will not be hard to find. You can check out the two registries of virtual reference services (Stephen Francoeur's site at http://pages.prodigy.net/tabo1/digref.htm and Gerry McKiernan's site at http://www.public.iastate.edu/~CYBERSTACKS/LiveRef.htm), review the archives of the two primary discussion lists in the field Livereference (at http://groups.yahoo.com/group/livereference) and Dig-Ref (at http://groups.yahoo.com/group/dig_ref/), or look at the exhibitor directories for the American Library Association's Annual and Midwinter conferences.

Bear in mind that there are also many software packages that have been developed for other purposes—such as e-commerce, help desk support, distance education, or just plain chat—that might be adapted for virtual reference. Adapting software from other fields can have its trials and tribulations—the companies you are dealing with won't know how you might use their software. The software may be designed for large applications and may not be available (or may be too costly) for the smaller installations used by libraries. You may not be able to expect much in the way of ancillary services such as database authentication, after-hours reference staffing, privacy protection, or other library-specific features. On the other hand, there is some great software out there, and many of the applications currently being used for virtual reference are modified versions of web contact center and chat software that was originally developed for other purposes. Who knows, maybe you will be the next one to discover some really wonderful software and adapt it for virtual reference. If you would like to explore software outside of the library field, you can put together a preliminary shopping list of software by checking out buying guides, directories, and review articles found on the websites of the trade publications for the call center, education and training, and web conferencing industries.

Once you've figured out what features you are looking for and put together a candidate list of software packages you'd like to review, follow up by visiting the company websites to find out more about the applications and see how they compare with your requirements. Request online demos from the most likely candidates, and ask each for a list of customer references you can contact. Finally, try to arrange for a trial or test period of a least a week or so for the software applications you are considering most seriously. Some of this software can be relatively complex, and it is difficult to fully explore all of its features or to gauge how well it will work for you without a chance to test it out rigorously.

If you are working with a consortium or contemplating a larger installation, you may be able to skip much of this discovery phase, and simply draft a request for proposal (RFP) specifying your requirements, and have the vendors respond to you. You may want to make a special effort to notify vendors outside the library field who may otherwise be unaware of your RFP.

How Much Staff Will I Need?

Although much of the attention in virtual reference circles tends to focus on the software selection process, in the long run, virtual reference staffing represents a far greater expense and a much more difficult problem to resolve. That's because opening up a virtual reference service is very much like opening up a brand new library. Unlike e-mail or other forms of "asynchronous" digital reference which could largely be handled in a librarian's "spare time," virtual reference services require that reference staff be at (or very near) a computer and ready to accept calls at all times the service is open. To further complicate matters, most libraries have found that it is extremely difficult, if not impossible, to staff virtual reference services from the regular reference desk, because walk-up patrons will routinely interrupt librarians typing on the computer on the assumption they are doing something that can wait. Also, the distractions of a busy reference desk can interfere with the focus and concentration you need to do virtual reference right. As a result, most libraries have found they need to dedicate staff specifically to their virtual reference service, and operate that service in an area well away from the regular reference desk. This is especially true as the service gets busy. Clearly it would be impossible to expect a librarian handling five or six virtual calls per hour (a rate already common in some of the busier virtual services) to help out much at the regular reference desk. In sum then, for planning purposes, it is best to create an entirely separate schedule for your virtual reference service, and assume that staff assigned to the service will be doing nothing else during the time they are at the computer. That way, when your service begins to grow, you can be assured you will have the staff to cover it, at least in the initial phases.

How do you calculate how many staff you will need? The number of reference staff required to run a virtual reference service (or any reference service, for that matter) depends on four factors:

1. the number of hours you need to cover;
2. the number of calls coming in;
3. the number of calls reference staff can handle simultaneously; and
4. the maximum number of consecutive hours any one person can be assigned to the virtual desk.

When you first launch your service, you normally don't need to worry too much about the number of calls coming in, since most services start off pretty slowly, and you have some control over the amount of traffic you get by the effort you put into marketing your service. So initially all you need to focus on is making sure you have adequate staff to have at least one person on the desk during all the hours you will be open. You don't need to worry too much about the number of consecutive hours staff spend on the desk at this point either, since traffic will be light, and staff will spend far more time waiting for calls than they will spend answering questions.

Calculating Call Volume

Eventually patrons will begin to discover your service, and you will need to begin to take traffic into account in calculating your staffing requirements. And since many of us in the library profession must start requesting new staff a year or more in advance, it is probably a good idea to give some thought to the potential traffic on your service and the staff you might need to handle it in your initial planning stages.

Up until now, calculating the number of librarians you need to staff a reference desk has been a pretty inexact science. Most of us who have managed reference desks, myself included, have simply asked for additional staff when we began to get reports that "it was getting busy out there" or when we began to see significant increases in the number of hash marks on our reference tally sheets. That "seat of the pants" approach to staffing works fine for a single reference desk where any increase in the number of questions coming in is likely to be relatively gradual, and where all you have to do is look at the length of the line at the desk to see if you have a problem. We usually lacked the data to do any more sophisticated analyses even if we had wanted to.

Unfortunately, our traditional approaches for guessing the number of staff needed at the reference desk don't work too well for virtual reference services. You can't just stick your head out of your office and look at the line at the desk, because the line is online, and it is always shrinking and growing as patrons are served, or hang up and others come in. Secondly, the number of questions coming into a virtual reference service can increase dramatically in a very short period of time. For example, traffic on the QandANJ service more than tripled after the *Philadelphia Inquirer* published an article on it. If you don't anticipate that sort of a jump and make sure you have adequate staff to handle it, you can frustrate your patrons and make your service and your library look bad.

Luckily, there is a more exact method of calculating staffing requirements for virtual reference services, and many of the software packages being used for virtual reference will give you all the data you need to use it. It is called the "Erlang C formula," and it was developed by Agner Krarup Erlang back in the early twentieth century for predicting the number of telephone operators required to handle a given number of calls. Today it is widely used to calculate the staffing needed in telephone and web call centers of all types (you could even use it to calculate the number of staff you should have on your regular reference service).

Here's the way it works. First you need to divide your virtual reference schedule into one-hour periods, and then either collect or estimate the following data for each one-hour period.

1. The average number of calls you expect in this one-hour period.
2. The average length of an online reference session in seconds.
3. The average length of time required to make notes, put away anything, and get ready for the next call (post-processing time).
4. The length of time you want your patrons to have to hold. This number is called the "service level" in the call center industry and is expressed as a percentage, as in, I would like to be able to answer 80 percent of the calls in 20 seconds.

Of course, those of you just starting out won't have your own data yet, so the following are some average figures compiled from over 150,000 reference sessions on LSSI servers to give you an idea of what you can expect.

1. *Average number of calls in a one-hour period.* This number can vary widely depending on a variety of factors, including whether you are running your service as part of a collaborative or independently, how much marketing and publicity you've done, the size of your service population, and probably other variables we are not yet of aware of. However, it is common for large collaborative services to generate anywhere from 20 to 30 calls or more, on average, during peak hours, and independent libraries could easily average 5–10 calls per hour during peak periods.

2. *Average length of an online session.* The average length of an online reference session runs about 13 minutes for both public and academic libraries across all libraries using the LSSI software. Anecdotal evidence indicates that this number is close to what others are finding as well.

Although there are a few extreme sessions that can run well over an hour, and others that are finished in less than a minute, most sessions tend to group pretty tightly around that 11–13 minute area. We are not quite sure why yet. Perhaps it is because the patrons or librarians tend to tire of chat after that period of time . . . or perhaps it is because the types of questions being asked online can usually be answered relatively quickly. It will be interesting to watch what happens to this number as we move ahead. In the meantime, you can be pretty safe assuming an average call length of 13 minutes, or 840 seconds.

3. *Post-processing time.* Libraries have not usually tracked how long it takes to clean up after one question and get ready for the next one . . . so most of us are still making pretty wild guesses on this one. If you don't have any data on it—and you probably don't—use 2 minutes or 120 seconds for purposes of estimation. This is based on the assumption that you may be classifying or writing up questions as you complete them. If you are not, you can reduce this time somewhat. The average post-processing time for the call center industry is 5 minutes, but that is probably a little high for us, since call center agents are normally required to complete order forms, update customer records, and perform a number of other tasks that are not necessary for reference.[1]

4. *The length of time you want your patrons to wait on hold.* This is another statistic we've generally ignored in the library world . . . but it is very important in virtual reference services to our patrons who are on the other end of the line. The rule of thumb for telephone call centers that want to provide really great customer service is that 80 percent of the calls should be answered within 20 seconds. There is some possibility that patrons are willing to wait somewhat longer to talk with somebody on the Web because there are other things they can do while they are waiting . . . but you can't go wrong using the 80 percent in 20 seconds rule for estimating your staffing requirements. If you are trying to run your service with less staff than you need, this is where your patrons will feel it first, because hold times will increase if either your questions increase or your question-handling time increases and your staff does not increase to match it.

To use the Erlang C formula, you can calculate it yourself following the directions given below (see figure 2-1).

If using this formula seems a bit daunting, you can use one of the many Erlang C calculators available on the Web. My personal favorite is

Figure 2-1 Erlang C formula

$$P(>O) = \frac{\dfrac{A^N e^{-A}}{N!} \quad \dfrac{N}{N-A}}{1-P + \dfrac{A^N e^{-A}}{N!} \quad \dfrac{N}{N-A}}$$

Where:

P (>) = probability of delay
A = total traffic volume of calls arriving measured in erlangs (e)
N = number of customer service officers available

on the Preferred Solutions Call Center Directory site at http://www.pref-solutions.com/html/calc.htm, but if that is not available, just use any general search engine and type in "Erlang C calculator," and you'll find many others.

So let's suppose you are extremely successful with your new virtual reference service. You do a great job marketing it; you've got links to it in your catalog and your databases; and you get the faculty to push it in class, or maybe you get it on the city hall page if you're a public library. People are beginning to log on in droves. And you've gotten to the point where you are regularly averaging 15 calls per hour on weekday evenings from 6 p.m. to 10 p.m. Now the question is, how many staff would you guess it would take to handle that volume? If you estimate this using the traditional "seat of the pants" method, you'd probably take the average number of calls you're expecting (15 per hour), multiply it by 13 to get the total number of minutes somebody will be on a call, and then divide it by 60 minutes to get the number of staff required . . . which, if you have been following along, would be 3.25. But if you run the same figures using the Erlang C formula, you would find that you actually need 8 librarians . . . more than twice as many staff as you had predicted using the simple approach. This is because the Erlang C formula accounts for the fact that calls will not be distributed evenly over that hour. There may be times when nothing is happening at all, and others when you may have five or more calls on hold at the same time. If you want to keep your hold times within reasonable limits, you need to have adequate staff to handle those peaks, even if it means you are a little overstaffed for the valleys. Erlang C gives you the tools you need to more accurately calculate your staffing requirements. This will become increasingly important as your service grows.

One further element you'll want to keep in mind in estimating your staff requirements is that many of the virtual reference software packages on the market allow you to work with more than one patron at a time. Some vendors claim that their software allows you to easily handle 3–4 patrons at a time, and one application even allows you to handle as many as 16 sessions simultaneously. However, it would be wise not to rely too heavily on this feature. There is no doubt that chat makes it possible to handle more than one patron at a time under some circumstances, but realistically speaking, most librarians have found that it is difficult to handle more than two patrons at once, even under the best of circumstances. We are not alone, either. A recent *Forrester Report* on chat confirmed that most customer service agents find it difficult to handle more than two customers at once.[2] If you are using the phone or voice over IP to talk with your patron, you will automatically be limited to a single session at a time. So while the ability to deal with multiple patrons can help relieve some of the pressure to add new staff as your service grows, be careful not to count on it too much, at least until there is better data on how well it might work in reference service.

So far we've used figures for expected call volumes, average call lengths, and desired hold times to calculate the number of librarians required to handle the traffic you could expect during any hour your service is open. The problem is that calls do not come in evenly over the course of a day or week . . . and librarians can't work an unlimited number of hours, either. So to calculate the actual number of librarians you'll need to staff your virtual reference service, you will need to set up a projected schedule. I would recommend you use a weekly schedule, because reference traffic tends to fall into a weekly pattern.

First, block out all of the hours in the week your service will be open. Next, indicate the average number of calls expected for each hour. You can either get this data from your own statistical reports if you already have a service, or by asking other libraries that have similar patterns of use, or just by wild guessing. Next, enter the number of staff you think you'll need to handle the traffic you expect for each hourly period. You are safe to assume a single staff member for hours when your predicted traffic is very low—say, five calls or less per hour. However, you should use Erlang C to calculate your staff requirements for all higher traffic hours. You should now have a weekly schedule listing your coverage requirements by hour. Now, use that data to put together a projected staffing schedule, just as if you were scheduling a regular reference desk. Obviously, you'll want to be careful not to schedule any one staff member for more than 40 hours per week . . . but you'll also need to give some thought as to how many consecutive hours and how many total hours you want to schedule your people to work the virtual reference desk. At this point, it is difficult to recommend any specific policy for number of hours at the desk. There are some librarians who do virtual reference 8 hours per day, 40 hours a week . . . and like it just fine. Other libraries will never schedule staff on the virtual desk for more than two hours at a time. However, the evidence indicates that handling questions online is a lot like working at the regular reference desk. So, if you have no other data to go on, start by adopting the policies you use to staff your reference desk to staff your virtual service—and see how things go.

If you made it through this discussion, you should now have a model schedule that will show you how many staff you need to cover your service for a particular level of traffic and for particular hours of operations. Because staff is such a large part of the cost of any reference service, virtual or otherwise, it is probably a good idea to update your estimates frequently and keep a close eye on this area as your service grows.

What Else Will I Need to Get Our Service Started?

So far, we've discussed various models for running virtual reference services, software features and selection, and how to calculate your staffing requirements. These are the major factors in the design of any virtual reference service. But there are other issues you may need to consider, depending on the type of service you are operating, who you are working with, what type of software you are using, how you intend to market your service, and other characteristics that vary significantly from library to library and service to service. Here, in no particular order, are some of the more common issues you may need to address in your particular service design.

SERVICE POLICIES

These include everything from which kinds of patrons you are going to serve, how you are going to answer questions, guidelines for the length of time to spend on a question, how to handle questions that can't be fully answered online, how to deal with harassing calls, and a slew of other issues. You are likely to find that many of the policies and procedures you have established for your regular reference desk will work just fine online. Be careful about trying to put too much policy in place in advance. Start with what you think will be minimally necessary and make up the rest as you go along. Overdoing policy can be a particular problem for an area as dynamic as virtual reference. So it is best to move slowly in this area.

COPYRIGHT

This is a policy issue as well, but it comes up often enough that it is best to address it separately. What types of material can be sent to which patrons without violating the letter or the spirit of the copyright law or the licenses you may have with database vendors? Virtual reference is new, and so there is no definitive legal interpretation in this area. As a result, libraries have been all over the map on how to handle this issue. Some require that patrons be authenticated before they will escort them into subscription databases, and they refuse to scan and send printed material out of their collections to anyone online. Others feel that working with a patron online is exactly like working with them in the library. So, if their database licenses permit in-house use to anyone who walks in the door, they feel that this likewise permits them to escort a patron into these databases online. Where you draw the line on this issue is up to you, at least until we have more definitive legal interpretations. Many libraries have found that the policies they set up for faxing and handling copyright materials at the regular reference desk can be easily translated online . . . so you might want to start by reviewing your policies in this area.

Collaboratives face a particular problem with copyright, because a group of libraries that often have different databases and online resources are sharing the same virtual reference desk. The question is, can a library share its online resources with patrons from other libraries in the collaborative? Libraries have come down on both sides of this issue. Some require that proprietary databases be used only with authenticated users of the library that owns them. Others feel that proprietary databases can be shared with any patron on the system, assuming that patron would also have been provided access to those databases if they had walked through the library door. There is no right answer yet, so you will have to be the judge.

ONLINE RESOURCES

If you will be doing reference online, you want to make sure you and your patrons have the best resources available to answer a question, and that they are easy to find and use. Many libraries have begun to purchase online ready-reference tools like Xrefer, online encyclopedias, a good general periodical database, the *Encyclopedia of Associations* online, and other tools that can help them answer a broad range of questions quickly. Also, collaboratives have often found it useful to purchase a few common tools expressly for reference use, ones that any member of the collaborative may access as long as they are in a virtual reference session. Many of the major database vendors have been willing to work with this approach, and it is particularly useful for collaboratives that do not share databases among their members. Finally, because it is important that reference staff be able to find the right content online quickly and easily, many libraries have set up special "ready reference pages" that include links to databases and to good ready reference sources on the wide open Web. The key to answering questions effectively online is easy access to good information.

PATRON INTERFACE

The design of the patron interface and log-in screens is a key element for many libraries and is well worth any time you spend on it, because the easier and more comfortable you can make virtual reference for your patrons, the more likely they are to use it. What you can do with the patron interface depends on the sort of software you are using. Some packages allow you to set up elaborate interfaces to authenticate the patron, ask a variety of questions at log-in, and route the call to different libraries or librarians according to the type of information requested, or according to the type of patron. For example, some libraries have set up different interfaces for children and homework help than those they use for their standard reference service. Some libraries have taken advantage of the patron interface to let prospective patrons know about their virtual reference service, what they can expect, and how to resolve common technical problems. Others are looking at putting knowledge bases or even automated bots in front of their virtual reference systems in the hope that some patrons may be able to find the answer to their questions on their own before they log in to ask a librarian.

Finally, the patron interface can play a key role in the marketing plan for your service. Many libraries, particularly those operating in collaboratives, have found it useful to create a whole new log-in for their service in addition to linking off the library website. Like Cleveland's KnowItNow service (www.knowitnow24x7.net) and the Bay area's QandACafe service (www.qandacafe.com), these services often have distinctive names with easy-to-remember URLs so patrons are not forced to remember long and arcane library web addresses to find the service. These virtual reference portals can make it much easier to advertise collaborative services because you can run an ad or a newspaper story and refer interested patrons to a single address rather than having to recite the names and web addresses of each participating library.

As you can see, there are many things you can do with the patron interface for your reference service, and you should be careful not to overlook it, or what you can do with it, as you design your service.

These are a few of the more common issues and concerns that will arise as you begin to develop your virtual reference service, and you are sure to run into many others that are specific to your type of library, your institution, and all sorts of local conditions. However, there have now been enough libraries that have gone down the road before you, that you are sure to be able to find somebody who has already had to deal with any issue that can come up, no matter how weird or esoteric it may seem to you. If you do run into something you can't figure out yourself, ask on one of the virtual reference discussion lists, and you are almost certain to find someone who has been through it before and is willing to give you a hand.

How Much Is All This Going to Cost?

The final, and sometimes the most important issue in designing a virtual reference service is how much money it will require to build and operate it. Of course, it is impossible to provide a definitive answer, because so much is dependent on the type of service you want, the type of software you are using, the hours you want to operate, the staff you are going to use, the amount you want to spend on marketing, and whether you are intending to go it alone or to join in with a collaborative—plus a host of other factors. However, it is possible to give you some guidelines for what you can expect in a few key areas, and that should be enough to help you make some decisions about the type of service you want and can afford.

SOFTWARE

Virtual software costs can range from completely free—if you adopt one of the instant messaging platforms like AOL, Yahoo, or MSN—to $100,000 or more for sophisticated web contact center software installed locally on your own hardware. That said, most virtual reference software is sold on an annual subscription basis, and the cost can range anywhere from about $2,000 to $6,000 for each simultaneous log-in by a librarian (typically called a "seat"). Because these "seats" can be shared with many libraries, the cost of these systems per library can be quite low when they are purchased as part of a collaborative. Some software vendors do not sell their software by seat, but instead sell it by the library (with an unlimited number of users), or by a profile—which could either be a library or a group of libraries—with the cost per library or profile ranging anywhere from $2,000 to $10,000. In some cases, these vendors can offer attractive prices for a single library, but they may be quite expensive for collaboratives, since each participating library has to buy in separately. Then there may also be separate training and installation fees that can add significantly to your first-year costs for either model. Bottom line, software costs can range anywhere from free to $25,000 for a typical single library installation, and from free to $3,000 or more for each library in a collaborative service. In both cases, it depends very much on exactly what type of software you get, and what sorts of ancillary services and training you want along with it.

REFERENCE SERVICES

As we discussed earlier in this chapter, many libraries that are operating 24 hours per day are doing so with the help of a commercial reference service that answers questions during the overnight and weekend hours when your staff are at home in bed. These services are brand new to the library market, and the few that are out there are experimenting with pricing, so whatever I say here is subject to change. The most common model is to sell reference services on a per question basis ranging from about $9 to $15 per question (which is significantly less than the cost per question calculated in many "in library" reference studies, by the way). Questions are normally sold in bundles of at least several hundred questions. The cost of a minimal package might be 500 questions at $15 each for a total of $7,500. The other pricing method is to charge a flat fee per student for academic libraries or per registered borrower for public libraries. Prices for this model range from $1.50 to $8 or so per student FTE or registered borrower, and the advantage of this approach is that the library pays a flat fee no matter how many questions are asked, while the vendor assumes the risk that patrons may ask more questions than it bargained for.

STAFFING

Staffing is a very real cost for any virtual reference service, and one we will all have to deal with eventually if these services grow and are successful. However, since most libraries start their services using existing staff, these costs are hidden and do not need to be budgeted for until the service grows to the point where you actually need to add staff to cover it. The one place where staff costs actually do show up in the budget is the salary for a project coordinator and maybe an assistant who are usually required to manage the operations of a collaborative reference service. However, there are very real staff costs in running any virtual reference service, and even if you don't see them initially, you will need to be concerned about covering them down the road.

RESOURCE AND DEVELOPMENT COSTS

Don't forget to include the costs of any additional online resources, web development work in setting up patron interfaces and the like, and any hardware you may be purchasing for your virtual reference librarians. These costs will vary depending on what you feel you need to buy, but it is important not to overlook them when you are figuring out your virtual reference budget.

MARKETING

The evidence we have so far indicates that you cannot spend enough on marketing, no matter how much you budget. So budget as much as you possibly can in this area, and then use each dollar you have budgeted as wisely as you can. The success of your service probably depends more on marketing than on any other single factor we have considered. I cannot emphasize this point enough. For further details on how you might spend these dollars, see chapter 4.

As you are adding all these costs up, don't forget that there are many ways to set up an effective virtual reference service, so if you come up with a cost estimate that doesn't seem to fit in the budget you have available, consider joining with a collaborative instead of going it alone. Or start off with free software and plenty of volunteer librarians and see what you can make of it. The most critical consideration for virtual reference services is not the software, or the resources you make available, but the number of hours you operate and the amount and effectiveness of your marketing. If you have plenty of librarians who are willing to contribute their time and you also have some novel approaches to marketing, you may be able to get both of these key components for little or nothing.

If you worked your way through all the details of this chapter, you should have the information you need to design an effective virtual reference system. The next step is to figure out how to run it, which we will take up in the next chapter.

NOTES

1. Average post-processing time in the call center industry, according to Benchmark Portal, at www.benchmarkportal.com.
2. "Chat Plugs a Customer Service Gap," *Forrester Report*, September 2002.

CHAPTER THREE

Managing Virtual Reference Services

In 1876 Samuel Swett Green laid the foundation for reference work in libraries when he wrote that "personal intercourse and relations between librarians and readers are useful in all libraries."[1] We might express it a little differently now, but more than a century and several technologies later, reference is still about personal relations between librarians and readers—regardless of whether the patron is standing in front of us at the desk, calling us on the phone, or chatting on our library website. The fundamental principles that served us well behind the desk will continue to serve us well online.

On the other hand, as more and more libraries have jumped into virtual reference service over the past few years, people have begun to raise interesting questions about how some of those fundamental principles might be best realized online. For example, are certain librarians better suited to virtual reference than others? Can you do virtual reference effectively from behind the regular reference desk? What's the best way to train staff to do reference online? How should we evaluate virtual reference services? Is it fair to use transcripts to evaluate the work of virtual reference librarians, and if so, what is the best way to do that? And new issues are coming up every day.

There are no definitive answers to any of these questions yet. The field is still very young, and most of us are making it up as we go along and libraries experiment with different approaches to managing virtual reference services.

INTRODUCING KAY HENSHALL AND MICHELLE FIANDER

However, some of us have been making it up longer than others, and so in this chapter I rely heavily on the advice and commentary of Kay Henshall, chief virtual reference trainer at LSSI, and Michelle Fiander, manager of the Web Reference Center at LSSI. Both Kay and Michelle have extensive experience in the field.

Kay Henshall has been training librarians in the mysteries of virtual reference since 1999, first as the project manager of the QandACafe virtual reference service in the Bay Area, and then with LSSI. By the most conservative estimate, she has trained over 2,500 public and academic reference staff on virtual reference over the past three years.

Michelle Fiander developed one of the earliest academic virtual reference projects, at the Indiana University, Purdue University at Indianapolis, and now manages the largest virtual reference call center in the world, with a total of 18 librarians who together handle an average of over 300 questions per day.

Neither Kay nor Michelle would claim to know all the answers, but they do have some well-informed opinions and are well qualified to provide an overview of the state of the art in managing virtual reference services, what has worked, and what hasn't. So let's get started.

WHERE SHOULD YOU DO VIRTUAL REFERENCE?

One of the first things you need to consider when setting up a new virtual reference service is where the librarians are going to work. Virtual reference technology allows you to offer the service from anywhere you have a computer and a decent connection to the Internet. Libraries have been experimenting with various locations with varying degrees of success.

The easiest choice is to run your virtual reference service from your regular reference desk, where you can take advantage of existing staff and where you have ready access to the print reference collection for those questions that can't be answered from online sources. However there are also some drawbacks to doing virtual reference at the desk. Virtual reference requires a fairly high degree of concentration, and the regular reference desk can be a distracting place. To a walk-up customer a chat session looks just like typing on a computer, and they will not hesitate to interrupt you. Moreover, librarians sometimes have to leave the desk to work with a patron and leave the computer unattended—and of course, it is usually right at that moment that a patron decides to log on from your website. Libraries have found effective ways to address these issues, however. Some libraries place their virtual reference terminal so the librarian is facing away from the desk when they are on a session, and one library even claimed that its librarians wore a sign saying "Please don't bother me, I'm doing chat reference," to keep walk-up patrons from distracting them in the middle of a session. It is easier to handle virtual reference on a desk where you have two or more reference staff on at the same time; that way there's a better chance someone will be available to work with walk-up patrons, and someone can stay at the desk to cover the computer when other staff are off in the stacks.

Of course, handling virtual reference at the desk is only an option when your service is small and you are only getting a few calls a day. Once your virtual service grows and you are averaging five or six web calls an hour or more, your virtual staff will be fully occupied and you will probably want to move them to a separate location, as they will be too busy to be of use at the reference desk.

The ideal location for a virtual reference service is a telephone reference center, if your library is lucky enough to have one. Telephone reference centers normally have a small group of staff that can be trained to handle phone or virtual reference service. Also, telephone reference centers usually have a good ready-reference collection designed for easy access, so questions can be answered easily and quickly if you need to go to print sources. The staff are already tied to their desks answering phones, so you won't need to worry about them wandering off into the stacks—and you don't have to worry about walk-up patrons interrupting them in the middle of a chat.

However, you can run into problems trying to merge virtual and telephone reference services. The most significant issue is that the phone routing system and your virtual reference software operate entirely independently of each other, which means that librarians may be routed a chat call when they are on the phone with another patron, and vice versa. This may be a manageable issue as long as your telephone staff is not too busy, and your online service is not generating a lot of traffic. However, when there are many calls, it can be difficult to keep track of who's next, and callers can be lost or left on hold forever. Some virtual software packages can be tied in with your phone system so that chat sessions can be routed along with regular phone calls—and the King County Library System outside of Seattle is working on this. However, it is neither cheap nor easy, and if you think you may be interested in doing this in the future, you will want to make sure that your virtual reference software and your phone system can work together. Check with a few call centers that have done similar integrations to see what is involved.

Finally, just because a librarian does well on telephone reference does not necessarily indicate that they will be successful online. In fact, many commercial call centers have reported that agents who do well on the phone do not always work well with chat, and vice versa.

If you don't want to use the regular reference desk and you don't have a telephone call center, your other option is to have librarians do virtual reference from their desks or from a special place you have set up for online reference. The advantage of doing virtual reference in a separate area is that you can set up an area that is convenient to the collection. A number of libraries have accomplished this by setting up a virtual reference center in a room near the reference desk. On the other hand, if you have librarians working from their own desks, they can do virtual reference and work on other projects at the same time, as long as those projects don't require them to stray too far from their PCs. On the downside, virtual reference can easily distract them from their other projects, and they may not have convenient access to the print collection. Of course, the big disadvantage to either option is that unless you hire additional staff especially to handle virtual reference—and very few libraries have been able to do this—by running your virtual reference system away from the regular desk or telephone reference service, you will be cutting into the time your staff had allocated to other activities and something is likely to suffer as a result.

One of the most attractive features of virtual reference software is that it has the potential to allow librarians to work from home, or from a hotel room overlooking the French Riviera, or from anywhere else they might want to be, as long as they have a good Internet connection, a computer, and a place to plug it in. Initially, libraries were skeptical of this approach because there was a feeling that librarians would need to be close to the physical reference collection in order to answer questions effectively. However, in practice this has turned out to be far less important than we thought. Most questions asked online can usually be answered with online resources, particularly if the software you are using allows you to share content from the library's electronic collections and databases. Even when a question cannot be fully answered online, it is often possible to give the patron a partial answer using online resources, and then offer to get back in touch with them later when you've had a chance to consult the print collection. As a result, doing virtual reference from home or some other off-site location has become an increasingly popular option among libraries. The LSSI Web Reference Center now operates almost exclusively with librarians working out of their homes. Other libraries are finding it a very effective way of providing after-hours service without having to keep the library building open, and it provides them with significant flexibility in scheduling because it is much easier to have a librarian log in for a couple of hours at home to cover a busy period than it would be to have them drive all the way to the library to cover it.

The major concern with off-site staff is to make sure that they have both adequate equipment and connections to handle virtual reference. The computer equipment will vary according to the type of software you are using, but it is usually a good idea to make sure staff has more than the minimal requirements, if you'd rather have your staff doing virtual reference instead of fighting technical problems.

The Internet connection is an even more critical issue. Although many virtual reference applications will work with a librarian on a 56k dial-up line, dial-up connections often go down or get interrupted in the middle of a call. So whenever possible, it is a good idea for off-site staff to have a cable connection or a DSL line. Moreover, since not all DSL or cable connections are created equal, you may want to have staff test the connection before they need to start relying on it. We know of several librarians who invested in high-speed connections that were so unreliable they could hardly handle e-mail, to say nothing of virtual reference. They were able to get their money back, but they could not work from home.

Of course, good computer equipment and high-speed connections can cost money, so some libraries have helped to subsidize Internet connections and sometimes even computer purchases for librarians working out of their homes. Others have purchased laptops specifically for their virtual reference project and checked them out to staff, and still others have asked staff who want to work from their homes to supply their own connections and equipment—so there is no consensus on how to handle this issue as of yet.

Finally, one note of caution regarding librarians working from home: many libraries and institutions have specific policies governing working from home and telecommuting, and you will want to familiarize yourself with these before going too far down this road, no matter how promising it may seem.

CHOOSING VIRTUAL REFERENCE STAFF

Now that we've looked at where you might want your virtual reference staff to work, let's take a closer look at just who you might want to have sitting behind those virtual desks, no matter where they might be located. What makes a good virtual reference librarian, anyway? And how do you go about accessing those skills?

As usual, there is no real consensus on this issue yet: some people are content to believe that a librarian is a librarian is a librarian, and that if staff can work well behind the desk, they should be just fine online. However, there is a growing perception that some people really do make better virtual reference librarians than others, and the fact that a person can do great reference behind the desk or over the phone does not necessarily mean they will be as successful online.

Characteristics of a Virtual Reference Librarian

We may not all agree on exactly what makes a good virtual reference librarian (I'm not sure we've really agreed on exactly what makes a good regular reference librarian either). But there is a group of characteristics that many people feel are important in how well someone will do with virtual reference, and you may want to keep these in mind as you select your staff.

Enthusiasm. A person's enthusiasm for virtual reference and your project may be one of the most critical factors in determining how successful they will be at providing the service. A person who is excited about what they are doing and interested in the project will have the resources they need to learn what they do not know, and be able to deal more effectively with the inevitable frustrations this new venue presents. On the other hand, nothing can be worse for a project than a librarian who does not believe in what they are doing and does not want to be there. They are unlikely to be able to adjust to new ways of doing things, and their bad attitude can drag the rest of your staff down with them. These people are likely to get caught up in a virtual reference project against their will when you require your entire reference staff to work the virtual desk whether they want to or not. A better approach would be to ask staff to volunteer for the project and then select your staff from those who really want to do it.

Quick on their feet. Virtual reference is a lot like ready reference: it encourages people who are quick on their feet, and have a thorough familiarity with sources, to get the answer out fast. Some people have suggested that the ideal candidate would be like Katherine Hepburn in the film *Desk Set,* but with great typing skills. Few of us are lucky enough to have anyone that good on our staff, but if you select librarians who are great at fielding those quick-answer questions people toss at us on the reference desk, they are also likely to do well with chat.

Good customer service skills. Remember that there is very little to go on in a virtual reference session, so the librarian must work extra hard to show the patron they are approachable and genuinely interested in helping the patron find the information they need. What this means is that librarians should bring good customer service skills to the virtual reference desk, and be willing and prepared to learn new techniques that may be necessary in chat—such as keeping in frequent contact with the patron. There should be no room for disinterested or surly reference librarians at any public desk, but even less so in virtual reference, where attitude can make all the difference.

Comfortable with technology. Much of virtual reference involves working closely with the computer and a variety of software applications to share information with a patron. Much of this technology is cutting edge, and libraries are often asking the software to do things it was never intended to do. Consequently, doing virtual reference often involves a good deal of hassling with the computer and the software and there will be plenty of times it crashes or just doesn't work. Someday we hope to have many of these issues worked out and everything should be easier to use, but for the time being, the more comfortable a person is using a computer and common software applications, the better they will be at dealing with the inevitable technical glitches when they develop.

Knowledge of electronic resources. A very high percentage of virtual reference questions are answered using online resources, and virtual reference patrons often opt for an electronic resource that is available right away, rather than wait for a better answer from a print source. This means it is important for would-be virtual reference librarians to be at least as familiar with the electronic resources available to them as they are with their print collections, and they should also be cognizant of electronic resources that can substitute for standard print titles . . . for those patrons who just can't wait. Of course, what's available electronically and in print is changing all the time, so it would be wise to arrange for regular training and refresher courses in this area, regardless of how well qualified your staff are to begin with.

Sample Application Procedure for Virtual Reference Librarians

It's one thing to define the traits and characteristics that make a good virtual reference librarian, and quite another to figure out who has got them. Of course, those of you who are planning to do virtual reference from the regular desk may not have too much choice about who you work with—which is one of the arguments against doing virtual reference using the regular desk. However, if you can swing it, it might be a good idea to have staff who want to work on the virtual desk go through a formal application procedure, similar to what you would use in hiring a person for a new position.

For those of you who are considering hiring new staff, or having existing staff apply for your virtual reference service, the following is an outline of the application procedure we use for prospective virtual reference librarians at LSSI. It may not be exactly what you need, but it should give you an idea of what to look for and where to find it.

All candidates for the LSSI Web Reference Center are asked to submit a resume and cover letter, and to take a timed online reference test. (The complete text of a "Sample pre-employment Screening Test and Key" is provided in appendix B.) We evaluate applicants on four basic criteria: resume and cover letter; performance on the pre-employment screening test; availability; and technical proficiencies.

RESUME AND COVER LETTER

The resume indicates the candidate's education and work experience. Librarians with an M.L.S. degree are preferred, but non-M.L.S. candidates with good reference experience and advanced degrees in other subjects, as well as a good service ethic, are also suitable candidates. Furthermore, we find that a candidate's lack of past experience doing reference work sometimes has little bearing on their ability to provide excellent virtual reference service. A number of candidates who have not done reference work ever or in years (for example, technical services people or systems librarians) have proved themselves able to do superior reference work. Don't judge a book by its cover.

The resume and cover letter also give an idea of the candidate's ability to express thoughts in writing; grammar and punctuation can be reviewed. The ability to write clearly is important in online reference because, at this point, chat is the primary means of communication. All online librarians make the occasional grammatical or spelling mistake, but librarians with generally poor grammar and problematic spelling make a bad impression for the virtual reference service.

PRE-EMPLOYMENT SCREENING TEST

The timed reference assignment is conducted via e-mail and must be completed within a two-hour period. The assignment includes two parts: part 1 focuses on the reference interview, and part 2 focuses on responding to reference questions. (See appendix B.) The candidate chooses a time to receive the assignment. The assignment is e-mailed at the appointed time, and the candidate returns it within the two-hour period. The e-mail's timestamp indicates whether or not the candidate returned the assignment within the two-hour limit. Setting a two-hour time limit on the assignment is done in an effort to make the candidate work under pressure. In online interactions, librarians must be quick to respond with some information or chat quickly and regularly in order to keep the patron engaged.

The assignment is based on actual questions posed to LSSI librarians. The goal of using "real" questions is to illustrate the variety of questions asked by online patrons. During the assignment the candidate does not have access to proprietary databases, but he or she is told which library the patron is associated with. The goal of this information is to indicate that Web Reference Center librarians will be responding to questions from more than one library or geographic area, and this will also be true for libraries working in consortia.

In part 2 of the test, each of the five questions requiring a response can be answered using freely available web resources. When a candidate does not find material to respond to the question, it indicates a number of things about his or her reference skills or reference approach, both of which are valuable to assessing a candidate's suitability for online reference work, or reference work in general. Candidates who find valuable resources which address the query, present these resources in context for the patron, and do so within the time limit are generally easier to train. Candidates who return the assignment early and do not find materials, but indicate the proprietary resources they would use, suggest that while they know databases they either do not know or refuse to use web resources. The candidates who fall into this latter category are not necessarily unsuited for online reference work. On the contrary, they often express a "Eureka!" type of response when presented with the key to the reference assignment. In the course of training they end up doing good work, and ultimately they do good work when working with real patrons. The interesting thing is that some librarians harbor a vague mistrust of free web resources, despite the fact that there is a terrific cache of authoritative information available free on the Web. Once these librarians are reminded of this, they are more inclined to use free resources when proprietary databases are not available. The reference assignment, then, does not serve to necessarily weed out candidates, but it does provide a way to quickly identify librarians with good reference skills, and it also provides us with a place to start as we approach the training and mentoring of those librarians.

AVAILABILITY

Depending on the hours of your service, a candidate's availability will play a greater or lesser role in his or her selection. In a 24/7 operation, it is clearly important to have librarians willing and able to work unusual hours. In the case of the Web Reference Center, a core of full-time librarians covers the bulk of the reference schedule, with part-time librarians used to provide backup and after-hours services. It is very important that librarians be available for minimum four-hour blocks of time at various times during the week, otherwise scheduling can become a nightmare.

TECHNICAL PROFICIENCIES

Candidates must be comfortable with the Windows environment and be able to navigate quickly. They should understand various e-mail, word processing, and notepad software packages. Ideally, the virtual reference software should become an extension of the librarian's hands so that their main thought processes can focus on the reference interaction, not on the technology. This is the goal, but it takes quite a bit of practice to get there. We don't expect people to get it immediately, but some of them do, and it's wonderful. Those who catch on quickly tend to be folks with extensive experience working with other software and applications. They are able to transfer their comfort from one piece of software to another.

TRAINING STAFF

Whatever method you use to select and hire staff, once you get them on board, the next step is to train them on the software and in the ways of virtual reference. Although some virtual reference vendors provide software training as part of their software offerings, the true scope of the training requirements is much broader than that offered by even the best vendors. In fact, training needs to be included as an ongoing and integral part of your virtual reference service from the very beginning, just as training has always been a critical underpinning of our regular reference services.

There is some debate about how best to provide virtual reference training, particularly among the online vendors. Some say on-site is best, others do it only online, and some claim their software is so easy to use you don't need any training at all. We'll let you make up your own mind about that. Whatever the case, software training is only one of many skills that librarians need to learn before they are ready to "go live." The following is a list of the areas you'll want to cover, along with some ideas about how best to train on them.

Virtual reference software. Librarians should know their virtual reference software backward and forward. It needs to feel like an extension of their own hands. I've read transcripts where it is very obvious that the librarian is extremely uncomfortable and wants to get rid of the patron as soon as possible because he or she doesn't feel confident using the software. The librarian needs to be thinking about how to answer the question, not what button she has to click to get the content to the patron. The patron will perceive this kind of behavior as rudeness and may never come back to use the service. Use whatever method of formal software training you choose, but be aware that to be truly effective, it must be coupled with lots of practice; enough so that the librarian ceases to worry about the software and is able to concentrate on reference service.

Electronic resources. Librarians need to be skilled at using electronic resources. Granted, not everything can be found on the Web, but in the virtual reference world, much of it needs to be accessed there. The whole reason the patron is using the service is to get some answers quickly. They don't want to be told that they will have to come in to the library. So if your librarians are not coming into virtual reference with a clear understanding of your databases and how to find information effectively on the Web, this is a great opportunity to train them.

Supporting hardware. Make sure everyone knows how to use any supporting hardware and software you are using for your virtual reference system. This includes knowing what to do with their computer when it freezes, crashes, or runs into some other common technical problem, as well as training on the use of scanners and scanning software that some libraries use to share their print collections. And don't forget question-tracking software, scheduling software, librarian-to-librarian back-channel communications, and other auxiliary software that is included in some virtual reference systems.

Windows operating system and Windows skills. (Those of you who have virtual reference software that works on other platforms can substitute Mac or Unix as desired.) Being able to work efficiently with virtual reference software means knowing how to use your operating system effectively. But it is surprising how many reference staff do not yet feel comfortable with some very basic functions. Before you place anyone on a live virtual reference desk, make sure they know how to:

- cut and paste
- toggle between multiple windows
- use "CTRL/ALT/DELETE" and the Task Manager
- use key commands, like "Windows M" (minimize window), "Windows E" (open Windows Explorer), "CTRL C/V" (copy and paste); and use the right click on the mouse to access the menu of commands

Customer service ethic. This is perhaps the most important factor in all reference work, and yet it is also the area that usually receives the least attention. We often hear comments like this in training: "Well, once I get them into the catalog or database or web page, I shouldn't have to spend a bunch of time showing them the information. They should have to do some of the work . . ." This attitude is dead wrong, and runs counter to the whole reason for doing virtual reference in the first place—to make it easier on the patron. If our reference numbers are dropping, the last thing we need is to force people to deal with surly librarians. On the contrary, we should be bending over backward for our patrons. We should provide them with a level of service that they can't get anywhere else. Customer service is the one area that we have control over. We can't control how Google improves its search engine, but we can control the personal touch that comes with working one-on-one with another person. This is the only area of reference where we can make ourselves indispensable. Resources will continually become easier to obtain, but having a conversation with another person who cares about your needs will never be available from a search engine. It is difficult to say how best to instill this attitude among your reference staff, particularly if they don't have it to begin with. However, it is important that you tackle this issue head on and make sure your staff is ready and willing to provide your patrons with great customer service. In the long run, the future of your service depends on it.

How Much Training?

Based on our experience bringing over 100 virtual reference projects online at LSSI, we find that libraries generally need to spend a day or two on the initial software training. Thereafter, librarians should plan to spend a minimum of about four hours per week practicing if they plan to "go live" in two weeks—which is a common expectation. We've found that it is wise to move training and practicing along at a fairly rapid rate, because the more time people have, the less inclined they are to get down to business and start practicing. That being said, a lot can be learned in trial by fire situations. If librarians have lagged on their practicing during the time leading up to their "go live" date, their learning curve tends to be very steep during the first few weeks they are live (provided, that is, the library has marketed effectively, and there is some traffic). This is not the ideal way to bring a service up, but the problem can be easily avoided if the project manager watches over the staff and makes sure everyone has enough time to practice before the service goes live.

How to Conduct Training

There are many ways to deliver training. The best way, of course, is to spend time with your trainees in person. We find that most trainees benefit greatly from a day or two of in-person training. However, a great deal can be accomplished by using the virtual reference software itself to deliver training to remote librarians. Depending on the capabilities of your software, slides can be "pushed" to participants in the class and trainers can monitor what is happening in the practice exercises—all while talking on a speaker phone in the room. We've found that it is difficult to train more than four or six people remotely at one time, and we also recommend keeping online sessions to one and a half hours or less—after that, both the trainees and the trainer tend to get tired.

The principles for training librarians in virtual reference are really no different than those for any other kind of training for adult learners. The training must be interactive and include many different kinds of materials to accommodate different learning styles. The techniques used in training include materials that are read, heard, seen, spoken, and experienced. The structure of the course should maximize participation and minimize lecturing.

How to Practice

At LSSI, we've found that online practice is best handled in stages. First, trainees can work by themselves on the same machine to become familiar with all the "buttons" and features, then they should progress to working side by side with a partner—watching the results of their actions. The next step is to work with a partner remotely to perfect their chat skills—not being able to talk to each other or see what is happening on the other end is much more realistic. At this point librarians should be paying close attention to the amount of time that passes between their messages.

As librarians train and practice on the virtual reference software, they progress through a variety of competency levels. What those levels are and the skills they represent will vary depending to some extent on the type of software you are using. Use the following scale of levels for general reference, and adjust them as needed to fit your own situation.

Virtual Reference Competency Levels

1. Knows how to use all the features of the software, outside of a live session
2. Can use all the features of the software in a live session (no time limitation)

3. Can toggle easily between chat and pushing pages/documents in a live session
4. Can use all the features of the software and maintain a conversation (no longer than 30–45 seconds between responses) with the patron
5. Can work at competency level 4 and answer questions effectively or come to a resolution (will e-mail back the information to the patron) in 20 minutes or less. This is not to say that all questions should be answered in 20 minutes. Actually, in most cases it should take less time than that, but as far as a competency level goes, this is a good starting point.
6. Can work at competency level 5 while assisting more than one patron at a time (working with more than one patron at a time requires a high level of skill and is rarely necessary in actual practice)

Mentoring

Once the initial start-up phases are over and your group grows in size, mentors become very important. You will need to identify reference staff who are catching on quickly and encourage them to become mentors. One project leader will never be able to keep up with everyone. If there are trainees who aren't catching on as quickly as others, you will need to be able to rely on your mentors to help pull them along. It's important to choose mentors by their skill at helping others, not just their technical skill with the software. Removing intimidation and fear from the learning process is half the battle when teaching any new technology.

Ongoing Training

Virtual reference training is never done, and in addition to informal mentoring and practice sessions, it is critical that you build an ongoing training program into your virtual reference service. Some of the most successful services hold regular refresher training sessions lasting one or two hours each month to cover topics like the following ones:

Skill refreshers. Trainees tend to remember only a small percentage of what they've learned in the classroom situation. Build in a little extra training on software features—particularly those that may not be used very often—to help increase and maintain skills.

New policies. Refresher training should also cover new policies as they are put into place. The new procedure must be completely understood and practiced. For example, when the Clevenet KnowItNow service started transferring health calls to advice nurses at the MetroHealth hospital, reference staff had to be trained to send the patron a scripted message, then send the patron a web page/disclaimer, and then transfer the call. This procedure was very important in order to protect the library from lawsuits, and it was critical that it be included in a formal training program to make sure everyone got the message.

Electronic resources. Electronic resource refreshers should take place when new database subscriptions are purchased or new usage policies are put into place. Especially in large consortia, librarians need to be well practiced at using the websites of all member libraries in order to match the patron to their resources quickly. And of course, their knowledge must also extend to the use of the resource once they get there.

EVALUATING VIRTUAL REFERENCE SERVICE

So far, we have looked at how to select your reference staff and how to train them on virtual reference technology and practices. But there is another major task in managing a virtual reference service—or any reference service, for that matter—and that is evaluation. This involves keeping tabs on how the service is running, and monitoring whether the staff and the reference service they are providing live up to your expectations.

There are three primary areas—we can call them "pulse points"—that you need to monitor to check on the vital signs of your virtual reference service: basic service statistics, patron satisfaction, and staff performance. Let's tackle these one at a time.

Basic Service Statistics

Most virtual reference software is capable of producing reams of statistical reports that can help you evaluate how your service is operating . . . and which should provide the raw material for thousands of library school projects in years to come. The specific statistics you have to work with will depend in large measure on the software you are using, but most packages should be able to provide you with reports to answer the following critical questions:

How many calls are you getting and when are they coming in? This is a critical measure of traffic, and ideally reports should show traffic on an hourly basis for each day of the week.

What is the median call length and how much do call times vary? This is also an important measure of service capacity, and you can plug it into the Erlang C formula (see chapter 2) along with your statistics on calls per hour to calculate your staff requirements.

How long are people waiting on hold, and what is your abandonment rate? This is another measure that will let you know when your service is reaching capacity. If customers are spending a long time on hold, or you have significant numbers of patrons who are hanging up before a librarian can pick them up, it is a clear indication that you need to add staff.

What is the trend? You should run reports on a regular basis—at least monthly, but weekly would be even better—and compare results as you go along. Comparing reports will help you identify trends in your statistics and enable you to take corrective action before you run into a problem.

What are the call resolution codes? Some virtual reference packages allow reference staff to classify questions by adding a call resolution code each time a virtual reference session is completed. This can be a very effective method of categorizing your questions according to subject or other criteria you may want to track, and you should take advantage of these codes if your software permits it.

Customer Satisfaction

It used to be that customer satisfaction was something we measured only sporadically, if at all, at the regular reference desk, but virtual reference changes all that. Many virtual reference applications have customer satisfaction surveys built in so they can be popped up or e-mailed to the patron immediately after every session. And if your software does not offer this feature, it is not difficult to make up something for yourself using standard web tools. No matter how you do it, it is now relatively easy to send each person who uses your service a survey to find out how they liked it.

Getting them to answer it, however, is another thing. Answer rates for these online customer satisfaction forms are averaging around 10–20 percent, and that means there are a great many patrons out there who don't care enough to respond. Libraries have tended to use long forms with lots of questions, and it is possible that patrons are discouraged by the length of the thing alone. Recently, a few libraries have begun to take pity on their patrons and shorten their surveys to three or four important questions that will fit in a single window without scrolling. It is too early to tell whether these short forms will improve the answer rate or not, but it will be interesting to see.

If you are going to do a customer satisfaction survey, it is important that you pay some attention to the principles of survey design before you start out. Much has been written on this area; but suffice it to say that far too many libraries throw something together without any real thought as to what exactly they want to measure, and the statistically valid ways of doing that. Another important design consideration is to make sure that your patron surveys can be linked back to a patron's reference transcript; the transcript can provide you with extremely valuable information about what happened in the session, and if things did go wrong, where they could be improved.

One final word of caution on patron satisfaction surveys: they almost always show librarians in a very good light. Often patrons will rank us at 95 percent or better, and even those who do mark us down might only drop our grade to a B or a B–, rather than flunking us altogether. I'm not sure that anyone has seriously investigated this phenomenon yet, but there is a good chance that much of it may have to do with the fact that our service is free, and patrons are easily satisfied with anything they get that they don't have to pay for. We might find quite different results if patrons actually had to pay for the service. Until we get a better understanding of what patron satisfaction means in virtual reference services, it is important the we pay attention to subtle nuances in the way people rank us, and not just glory in our high ratings. That means we should be looking closely at reference sessions where patrons rated us anything less than perfect, because they may be indications of problem areas.

Staff Performance and the Use of Reference Transcripts

Up until the development of digital reference services, evaluating the quality and efficiency of reference work had been a difficult and tricky process.

Most of the work we did vanished into thin air as soon as the patron left the desk, and the only way we had of appraising the overall quality of a librarian's work was reviewing the general comments of their peers and colleagues, as well as an occasional complaint or commendation from the patrons themselves.

This is not so anymore. For the first time in the history of reference, we now have a chance to see what we have done, because most virtual reference software documents everything we do in a session, from how long the patron waited on hold before we picked them up, to every line of chat, every nuance of expression, every web page visited, right down to how we said goodbye. It is all captured verbatim in a reference transcript—along with the name of the librarian and the patron involved, and with data from the patron satisfaction survey if your system has been set up to capture it.

Some reference staff find these reference transcripts a little scary. But many view them as a wonderful tool that we can use to improve the quality of our own individual performance and of reference services in general. And they are a very important—some might even say critical—tool that allows libraries working in collaboratives or using subscription after-hour or specialty reference services to evaluate the quality of the reference work being done in their name.

The question is, how do we best use these transcripts to evaluate and improve reference services? Who should be reviewing the transcripts? How many do you need to review and what should you be looking for? Let's start by taking a look at how you might review the work of other libraries or subscription reference services that are doing work in your name, because they are the simplest cases to handle.

Ideally you want the project manager, or a team assigned by the project manager, to go through and review all work done by outside reference services whether they are another library or a commercial reference service. At least in the early days of your project, it is a good idea to review each and every transcript completed, until you feel confident that the outside library or reference service is living up to your expectations—and as long as the total number is not unmanageable (wading through transcripts can be a time-consuming and arduous task). Once you are satisfied with the basic performance of the service, you may want to cut back a little on the number of transcripts you review, and perhaps just look at a random sample, plus any with lower patron satisfaction scores. It is also important to review transcripts in a timely fashion (once a week is good) so you can catch problems before they get too serious, and follow up while the events around a particular reference session are still fresh in people's minds.

It is best to make up a review sheet or evaluation form to help you keep all the criteria you want to evaluate in mind as you go through the transcripts. The criteria you consider and how you weight them will depend on what's important to you. To help give you an idea of what you might want to include, a sample of the transcript evaluation form we use at LSSI is provided below. You can modify it to suit your own purposes, or you can create your own.

Now that we have looked at the basics of how to use transcripts to review the reference work of outside libraries or vendors, the question is how should you apply those practices to your own virtual reference staff. In theory, the approach ought to be the same. After all, your reference staff is representing your library to your patrons and your community in the same way an outside library or a vendor does, and it would be a good idea to hold them to the same standards—I assure you the patrons certainly will. However, in practice, there is a difference. You can pull out of a collaborative when you don't like the level of reference service they are providing, and you can terminate a contract with a vendor at any point—but you have to live and work with your staff every day, and that may argue for a somewhat more cautious approach to reference evaluation and transcript review.

The objective should be to give your staff the feedback they need to improve the reference service they are providing—without embarrassing anyone unnecessarily, and also to commend those who have done an exceptionally good job. There are a variety of ways libraries can handle this. The first is to have the project manager review selected transcripts for all staff members and make notes on things that were done well and things that might be improved—and then to return them to each reference staff member privately. Another method is to strip identifying information off the transcripts and have the entire virtual reference team review them collectively. The advantage of this method is that it helps spread the review work out a little, while still protecting the "privacy" of the staff. Or you could provide each staff member with a copy of your transcript evaluation form and have everyone review and comment on their own transcripts; then you might have them share their analysis at a staff meeting so that

LSSI Reference Transcript Evaluation Form (Page 1)

Reviewer's Name: ____________________

Librarian's Name: ____________________

Queue: ____________________

Call ID: ____________________

Date of Transaction: ____________________

Time of Transaction as Follows:

Beginning Time: ____________________

End Time: ____________________

Total Time: ____________________

1. Answered? _____ Yes _____ No _____ Partially

1a. If response to no. 1 is No, please indicate—more than one may be selected:

_____ Patron disconnected before answer could be provided.

_____ Librarian disconnected before answer could be provided.

_____ Were technical difficulties indicated by either librarian or patron as reason for disconnect?

_____ Question too complex. Librarian offered to follow up.

_____ Other? Please explain. ____________________

____

General comments: ____________________

____

1b. If response to no. 1 is No or Partially, indicate how long the patron waited online:

_____ 5–10 minutes _____ 10–20 minutes _____ More than 20 minutes

2. Follow-up or Referral Necessary? _____ Yes _____ No

2a. If Yes to 2, was the referral or follow-up made? _____ Yes _____ No

2b. If Yes to 2, what type of follow-up? _____ E-mail by original librarian

_____ Referral to client library _____ Other (please specify)

LSSI Reference Transcript Evaluation Form (Page 2)

2b. Proper Call Resolution Code selected? _____ Yes _____ No
(If No, please suggest more appropriate Call Resolution Code)

3. Reference Interview: _____ Excellent _____ Good _____ Adequate _____ Poor
Why? ____
____

4. Communication/Explanation: _____ Excellent _____ Good _____ Adequate _____ Poor
Why? ____
____

5. Tone/Courtesy: _____ Excellent _____ Good _____ Adequate _____ Poor
Why? ____
____

6. Use of Client Library Resource, if Necessary/Appropriate? _____ Yes _____ No _____ N/A
Comment/suggest appropriate resource: ____________________________
____

7. Time Spent on Question:
Did the length of time spent on the question seem appropriate? If not, why not?
____

8. Spelling/Grammar: Correct and Coherent, for the Most Part? _____ Excellent _____ Good _____ Adequate _____ Poor

everyone can benefit from the exercise. Finally, you might try using a carrot instead of a stick, and establish some kind of reward for an exemplary virtual reference transcript and have staff submit their best efforts, in exchange for a chance to win a trip to a conference, or a few days off the virtual reference desk. I'm sure you can think up some other strategies without too much effort. The important thing is to realize the valuable insight these transcripts provide us into the reference process. We should be taking advantage of them whenever we can to help us improve the way we work.

OTHER DETAILS

In this chapter we have covered the major issues in managing a virtual reference service: where to do it, how to select and train staff, and how to measure and evaluate the service you are providing. Unfortunately, that's not all you have to worry about. There are a host of other details you will have to handle as you work to get your service up and running. However, many of these will be particular to your institution, or the software you are using, or some other local policy, condition, or issue. And there is no way we can even begin to address all of those. But there are a couple of minor matters that can turn into major irritants if they are not handled correctly, and I'd like to take a minute to address them in the hopes of saving you some grief down the road.

Scheduling

Reference scheduling was never very fun, even when we were just scheduling a single desk, and it can turn into a major problem when you are scheduling a virtual staff that may be scattered all over the landscape. It can get downright impossible when you are trying to keep track of the personal schedules and preferences of thirty or forty reference staff representing as many different libraries, as is the case in some of the larger collaborative services.

The solution is to use calendaring or scheduling software. If you have a small operation limited to a single library, you might be able to adapt one of the free calendaring programs like Yahoo Calendar, or something similar. You won't need anything too sophisticated, but it is good to have it on the Web, so that staff can pull it up and view it whenever they need to.

However, once you need to schedule a larger number of staff, or that staff is located in a number of different libraries, you'll want to start looking for scheduling software. What you want is a program that allows staff to put in times they are available, and their preferences, and allows you to specify the number of people you need to cover various hours. Then you push a button and the software schedules the staff for you and posts the schedule to the Web. Some programs will even allow staff to request days off or swap shifts online, and these features can be a real boon if you are scheduling a large number of staff over several different shifts. It used to be that scheduling programs were very expensive and only those projects with huge scheduling problems could justify their cost. However, costs have come down dramatically, and it is now possible to get a good scheduling program like ScheduleSource (www.schedulesource.com) or similar ones for less than thirty dollars per person per year—and they are worth every penny of it; just ask anyone who's tried to do it by hand.

Back Channel

Another option you'll want to consider is a "back" communications channel that allows reference staff who are online to talk or message with one another outside of a virtual reference session, and ideally outside of the virtual reference software itself. This can be very useful when staff need to contact one another to coordinate shift changes, alert each other to software problems, or just discuss a matter outside the "earshot" of the patron. Some software packages come with this feature built in; the only problem with this is that an internal channel is not too helpful if the problem you want to talk about is with the virtual reference software itself, and it often is. However, if your software does not come with its own back channel, or if you'd like your staff to have a way of talking with one another outside of the software, then you may want to consider setting everybody up on one of the commercial instant messaging services provided by AOL, Yahoo, or MSN. All you need to do is have all your virtual reference staff download the instant messaging software and add each other to their "buddy lists." That way everyone will be able to see at a glance who is online, and they will be able to message each other back and forth independently of your virtual reference software and any problems they may be having with it. Many libraries have used this approach very successfully for a number of years now, and it is very difficult to beat the price: it is totally free.

In this chapter, we've covered the basics of setting up a virtual reference service and the key factors in managing one; but as many libraries are finding out, all of your time, money, and effort will be for naught unless you take steps to let patrons know about your service and encourage them to use it. Even though the virtual reference phenomenon is still only a few years old, there are already services that have closed from lack of use, and if you don't want the epitaph on your service to read, "Suppose they built a reference service and nobody came," it would be wise to pay at least as much attention to how you market your service as to anything we have covered so far. And that's what we'll do in the next chapter.

NOTE

1. Samuel Swett Green, *American Library Journal* 1 (1876): 74–81.

CHAPTER FOUR

Marketing Virtual Reference Services

You can do everything else right. You can design the best virtual reference system in the world. You can purchase the most sophisticated software, and hire and train the most experienced staff, and buy them every reference tool imaginable. But I can assure you that no matter what else you do, or how much money you spend, your service is guaranteed to flop unless you pay sufficient attention to marketing. Think of marketing as the fuel that makes your service run. You can have the world's greatest aircraft, and the finest pilots and flight crew, but without fuel, you'll never get it off the ground. And so it is with virtual reference services. I wish I could tell you this was all based on conjecture, but the sad truth is that there are many libraries that have not paid sufficient attention to marketing, and even though virtual reference has only been on the scene for a few years now, some services have already been shuttered for lack of use. If you don't want yours to meet a similar fate, it's important to build marketing into your service from the ground up.

The problem is, libraries have traditionally shied away from marketing. This is partly due to the fact that, up until now, we've never really had to worry too much about it. Throughout most of our history, libraries have been the only place a person could turn to when they needed access to a book collection or when they had a reference question that couldn't be answered out of their own dictionary or encyclopedia. That monopoly, coupled with the fact that most library buildings are centrally located (either downtown or in the middle of a college campus), assured that most of those who needed our services would find us sooner or later. There was little need for librarians to spend precious money or time trying to attract attention.

All of that has changed with the advent of the Internet. We are no longer the only game in town. People have a variety of choices where they can turn for books and information, and libraries now have formidable competition. Our central locations that once served us so nicely do us little good on the Internet, where the library is but one among millions of competing sites—and often a pretty ugly one at that. So our traditional approaches—or should I say non-approaches—to marketing are not likely to work well for us on the Web.

Even libraries that recognize the need for marketing have been wary of it for a couple of reasons. First, many people feel it takes a lot of money to do an effective marketing job, and since money is always limited in libraries, they reason that it is better to do little or nothing if you can't afford to spend what it takes. Second, there is the fear of success. Some libraries are worried that if their marketing efforts do succeed, they will be overrun with more patrons than they can handle.

Both of these concerns are valid. Marketing can cost lots of money. Ask the National Library of Canada how much it spent to put its ad on television during the Stanley Cup hockey finals (Can$15 million). And it is possible to be overwhelmed with traffic—just ask the librarians at Q and A NJ what it was like after the front-page story on their service ran in the *Philadelphia Inquirer*. However, there are also some very affordable strategies for marketing virtual reference services, as well as effective methods of controlling demand if you are successful.

In this chapter, we'll take a look at some of the more interesting and affordable methods libraries are using to market their services, and also consider some innovative but untried strategies that seem to have potential. Most of these approaches are designed to fit within the budget of the average library, and some of the most effective methods cost little or nothing. In fact, there is really only one marketing strategy you cannot afford in virtual reference, and that is the strategy libraries have traditionally adopted—the strategy of doing nothing at all. This approach may have once worked for traditional reference services, and we could get away with it for e-mail reference services which involved no special software or training, and when it didn't take too much staff time to answer those few questions we received. But virtual reference services require substantial expenditures in software, staff time, specialized training, and resources.

You cannot afford to make those expenditures and commit your staff to sitting in front of computers for hours every day and have nobody show up. Lack of traffic is the kiss of death for virtual reference services. It has killed several already, and it will kill yours too, unless you pay proper attention to marketing.

SERVICE HOURS AND MARKETING

Before you start thinking about how you will market your service, and long before you set up committees to design your promotional bookmarks and coffee cups with logos on them, you'll want to make sure that you are offering your patrons adequate service hours. There is no point in spending large amounts of money and time trying to attract patrons if they are likely to find your service closed when they get there. Patrons expect reference services to be open when they need them, and they are unlikely to plan their day just so they can talk to a reference librarian between 2 p.m. and 4 p.m. on weekday afternoons, or some equally circumscribed schedule. So if you are going to offer virtual reference services, make sure that you offer them for a reasonable number of hours, and that the hours are predictable. Around-the-clock (24/7) operations are the best, and not because there are so many people wanting to ask questions in the wee hours of the morning. It is because 24/7 services are predictable. Patrons can count on the fact that a librarian will be there to help them any time of the day or night, and they don't need to give the schedule a second thought. However, if you cannot manage a 24/7 service, try to keep the service open as many hours as you can and make those hours as predictable as possible. If it is anything less than 24/7, try to set a schedule that best suits your patrons' needs—and these may vary from community to community. If you're not quite sure what your patrons might want, our experience at LSSI shows that virtual reference services are most heavily used from early afternoon until midnight. If that schedule is still a bit too much for you to manage, the next best choice would be a service that operates during the regular business hours of the library—it's not ideal, but it is predictable, and many of your potential patrons will already have at least a rough idea of when the library is open.

If you've taken a long look at your staffing and other resources, and find that you truly cannot afford to offer your service for more than a few hours a day, a few days a week, then it is likely that any money put into marketing such a limited service would only be wasted, because patrons will have a tough time trying to remember when you're open. Even if they can, there's a good chance their question won't wait until the next time they can get you live and online. You'd probably be better off using the software for planned bibliographic instruction sessions, author chat sessions, and other kinds of scheduled online programming rather than trying to run a full-scale virtual reference service. Or you might combine your e-mail and live services to create a web reference center where patrons could ask questions 24 hours a day, 7 days a week—in some cases librarians would be available to assist patrons live, in others they would ask their question via e-mail and somebody would get back to them shortly. It may not be the best configuration, but at least you're not asking your patrons to keep track of crazy schedules or creating unrealistic expectations about the level of service they can expect from you. No matter what you do, if you are going to spend money marketing your service to your patrons, it is important you do everything you can to make sure somebody will be there for them when they come to find you.

WHAT IS MARKETING?

Okay, you've got your service set up, you've made sure you're offering a reasonable schedule, and now you're ready to start marketing your service. But what is marketing really?

Although marketing is the subject of an enormous literature, thousands of courses, and entire academic departments—not to mention thousands of marketing firms and consultancies—nailing down a precise definition of it is easier said than done. For the purposes of this book, I would like to define marketing very practically as "letting people know about your service(s) and what you can do for them."

The problem is that not all people are alike. You serve all sorts of different people—faculty, grads, undergrads, alumni, users in the library, urban users, rural users, and ad infinitum. Each of these groups has different needs. Faculty may use your service primarily for citation checking, or when they are starting out on major research projects. Grads may want to set up consultations on their dissertation research. Undergrads may just want a couple of articles they can throw into their paper late Sunday night. Urban users may want some online homework help for the kids.

Rural users may need special document-delivery services because of their remote location.

Likewise, the marketing approaches you use to reach these different groups will vary. You might assign a librarian to personally introduce your new reference service to likely faculty, while taking a somewhat less personalized approach with students. Similarly, distributing bookmarks about your service through the local Barnes & Noble and Borders outlets might be a fairly effective method of reaching some urban users, but it is not likely to work too well in rural areas.

Therefore, the first step in developing any marketing program—whether for virtual reference services or orange juice—is to sit down and segment your users, to (1) figure out what groups of users you want to serve and what their various needs and wants are, (2) determine how your services can help meet those needs, and (3) identify marketing approaches that may be best suited to reaching each of your many audiences.

The user groups or segments you identify will differ from library to library. But there are two important segments that all libraries have in common:

the group of patrons who are already using your library services either through your website or inside your building; and

everyone else . . . i.e., those people who are not currently using your services and probably have never visited your building or your website.

Your current users are the easiest group to market to because they are already on your website and in your buildings. We'll assume they need what you have to offer, otherwise they wouldn't be there. The one thing they don't know about is your virtual reference service and how it can benefit them. But they are easy to reach with a variety of free or very low-cost strategies, so a small investment in marketing to this segment can pay off handsomely.

Those people not currently using your service are also an important group; many of us are setting up virtual reference services especially to attract this group. However, they are generally much harder to reach, and you will need to adopt different strategies and spend more money and resources to reach them. Reaching non-users requires a much more sustained effort before it begins to pay off. So while you will definitely want to include this segment in your plans, you should not expect immediate results and it will cost you more. Reaching non-users should probably be a second priority, especially for those of you just starting out.

MARKETING STRATEGIES FOR EXISTING LIBRARY USERS

Existing users are already familiar with your library and the services you offer. They are in your buildings checking out books. They use your catalog and databases. Many have discovered your library website and are accessing your services remotely. Most have probably seen your reference desk and some may have even asked a question there. There is no need to convince them of the value of your services; they are already well aware of that. The one thing they are not aware of is your new virtual reference service and the fact that librarians are available to help them live and online any time they need it. So your objective in marketing to this group is to let them know the service exists and how they can access it. Fortunately, virtual reference technology itself offers a number of free or very low-cost strategies for getting that message across.

The Ubiquitous Library Strategy

The ubiquitous library strategy simply means putting links to your service everywhere a patron might need help. It costs absolutely nothing, and so far it has proved to be the single most effective method of marketing virtual reference services, bar none.

The problem is that most libraries normally create only a single link to their virtual reference services, and that is often on a page that may be buried several levels down in the library website. So patrons who are browsing your site and need help must first remember that you offer virtual service, then they have to stop what they are doing and try to find your log-in page. Then, when they finally get to you online, they may have to return to the page they were working on and re-create their results so you can see where they went wrong. It is a cumbersome and time-consuming way to ask a question. Small wonder, then, that few patrons are willing to take us up on it.

There is no need to put your patrons through all of this trouble. Almost any virtual reference software currently on the market allows you to create as many patron entry points as you want at no additional cost. So it is very simple to create a link to your virtual reference service from every page on your library site, and libraries that have done so have generally seen a dramatic increase in use. The reason is obvious: the patron sees you have a reference service at the point they need help, and they don't need to leave the page or drop what they are doing to access it . . . they just click on the link. A further advantage is that some software packages will automatically send the page the patron is on to the librarian when they first enter the session, which makes it easy to see what the patron was trying to do when they asked for help.

Bear in mind that all links are not created equal. Try to make the links to your service as prominent as possible on your pages (don't bury them as tiny "Help links" in headers and footers), and adopt a service name and logo that patrons will remember. "Ask a Librarian," probably the most common service name out there right now, may explain the process, but it is hardly inspiring or memorable. Try to come up with something a little more distinctive that will stick in the patron's mind the next time they need help. Cleveland's KnowItNow service, New Jersey's QandANJ, and SeaWorld's AskShamu are several good current examples.

It is easy enough to increase the links to your service on your own web pages, and doing so can generate a significant increase in traffic. But the results are even more dramatic if you can place links to your service inside your catalog and databases, because these are precisely the areas where your patrons are most likely to need your assistance. However, since libraries often have little or no control over the patron interface for their catalog or databases, finding effective methods to get your service in front of your patrons when they are in these proprietary interfaces can be a little trickier. Catalogs tend to be a bit easier to work with, and a number of them, including Innovative Interfaces, allow you to add links to your service in the page headers and footers. A few vendors—Gaylord and Sirsi, for example—have taken this a step further and are actually building "smart catalogs" that actively incorporate virtual reference technology. These catalogs will actively suggest reference assistance when a search has turned up zero results or too many results, and they also allow patrons to log on automatically using the patron profile from the catalog database, and to track their reference questions online. Although the concept is still quite new, libraries that have managed to get their service inside the catalog have reported major increases in usage. Of course, some of that new traffic is patrons asking circulation-related questions, but that just means you need to get your circulation department involved in your virtual reference service as well. Many of the virtual reference applications will allow your circulation and reference departments to work together very effectively online.

Things have not moved along as quickly with databases. Some vendors have built e-mail links inside their interfaces which can be used to link to virtual reference services, and some allow a degree of customization on their search and results screens. Libraries that mount the databases on their own servers or who use third-party gateways such as WebFeat, Muse, and others may have enough control over the web interface to integrate their virtual reference services. On the plus side, as of this writing, I know that a number of database vendors are actively considering developing "smart database" models similar to those found in some of the leading-edge catalogs . . . so if we can't access virtual reference services through many of our databases right now, there is a very good chance we will be able to do so in the not too distant future.

The Persistent Button

Another way to ensure that your service is available to your patrons anywhere they might need help is to place a link to your service directly on their browser or as an icon on their computer desktop. This is generally known as the "persistent button feature" and it is offered by a number of virtual reference vendors, including both Convey and LSSI. If your vendor doesn't offer it, the desktop icon is pretty easy to create for anyone with a little programming skill. The persistent button works like this: the patron downloads a small applet (usually less than 10k), and that applet places an icon for your reference service on the patron's desktop or, in the case of Convey and LSSI, directly on the patron's browser bar. The desktop icon is there all the time. The Convey and LSSI buttons can be programmed to appear only when the patron is browsing certain domains that the library has specified; in other words, you can program the button to appear when your patron is browsing in your databases or using Google (places where it might be pretty tough to get links to your reference service under normal circumstances). When patrons have a question, all they do is click on the icon and it connects them directly with your service. If they are using the desktop icon, it automatically launches their browser and connects them to your service. The button stores the patron information so log-ins are automatic, and patrons do not have to waste their time filling in their name, e-mail address, and the like. The advantage of the "persistent button" is that it allows you to keep your service in front of your patrons even when they are working in areas—like databases—where it is otherwise difficult to get links, and even when they are browsing in totally separate areas of the Web. Your service is always represented with the same icon and appearance, something that can be pretty difficult to achieve when you are adding links to databases and catalogs. The downside to the button is that it does require the patron to accept a download, and many of them may not be willing to do so. However, if it is a small download and it is an optional feature that is not required to take advantage of the basic functions of software, patrons may be more willing to accept it.

Proactive Chat

So far we have looked at marketing techniques where the objective is to make your service more accessible to your patrons, but in each of these cases, it is still up to the patron to initiate the session. Some do, of course, but there are still many visitors to your library website who may choose not to ask for help, even though you've done everything you can to make the option available to them—just as there are many people who use the library, but who never stop by the reference desk and ask a question, no matter how much they might be able to benefit from our help.

Recently a number of e-commerce sites have grown tired of waiting for customers to contact their sales agents, and they have begun working with software that allows them to initiate a live web session with the customer.[1] This feature—sometimes called "proactive chat"—is also available in some of the virtual reference applications used in the library market, including Groopz and LivePerson. It works like this: the software allows a librarian to monitor users as they navigate your website. When it appears a patron might need some help, the librarian can launch a window on the patron's browser that asks if they need help. If the patron responds, the system automatically brings them into a live reference session.

Businesses that have begun adopting this strategy have found that it can increase the number of customers they chat with on their websites (about 3.5 percent of the patrons visiting the Technoscout website end up in chat sessions using the proactive technology), but it raises some serious privacy issues for most librarians. Even though many of us have been doing "proactive reference" for years—that is, we will ask a patron who seems to be lost in the stacks if they want some help—that still seems a little different from watching a patron's every movement as they go through your library website. Since the patron has no idea they are being watched, floating a little "Can I help you" balloon in front of them may startle and put them off more than it encourages them to ask a question. However, proactive chat is clearly a strategy that has met with some acceptance in the business world, and it might work for libraries as well if we can find ways to address some of these issues.

Advertising to Existing Users in the Library Building

All of the marketing strategies we've explored so far assume that your patrons are already coming to your library's website, and all you have to do is entice them to ask a question. However, there is bound to be a certain percentage of your current patrons who have never visited your website, and may not even be aware you have one. Reaching these people presents something of a different problem than marketing to patrons who are already on your website. You will really need to explain your virtual reference service as part of an entire package of services that the library offers online. In fact, marketing to these patrons is a lot like marketing to the public at large—with two major exceptions: (1) they are already familiar with the resources and services your library offers inside the building, and (2) they are already coming into your building, so they are much easier to reach than the public at large.

This means you should take full advantage of your library building and all your current programs and activities to help promote your virtual reference service and the rest of your online services to your patrons. There are hundreds of different ways to do this, and libraries are coming up with new ones every day, but here are a few of the more useful or interesting approaches that you may want to consider.

Bookmarks and premiums. This is by far the most common in-house marketing technique. Distribute them at reference, circulation, and other service desks . . . and at the campus bookstore too, if it will accept them. If you want to spend a little more money, libraries have ordered all sorts of imprinted items including coffee cups, pencils, flashing buttons, rulers, book bags, and notebooks to advertise their service. It just depends on how much you want to spend.

Routine correspondence. Tout your new virtual reference service on all the mailings that get sent out regularly to patrons. This includes hold notices, overdue notices, and other things you send out on a regular basis.

Library welcome packages. Of course, you will want to include a nice flyer or brochure about your virtual reference and other online services in a "welcome" or introductory packet that comes with each new library card.

Banners. I know of at least one library that strung a huge banner announcing its new virtual reference service over the building's entranceway. It was hard to miss that, and it didn't cost very much either.

Library programming. Have your virtual reference service "sponsor" some of your regularly scheduled library programming; that will give you a chance to say a few brief words about the service at the beginning of the program, then the audience can go on to hear about Mark Twain or the *Canterbury Tales* or whatever else would regularly be discussed. Even better, if your software permits it, you might offer to "simulcast" some of those programs online, so that remote patrons could attend and be introduced to your reference service at the same time.

Bibliographic instruction. It goes without saying that you would want to include information on your service in all of your bibliographic instruction and database training sessions. It is a great idea to include a live demo when you can. And if you want to get really innovative, why not hold some of those bibliographic instruction sessions online (assuming again that your software supports online meetings)? Students may appreciate the opportunity to get educated from the comfort of their dorm rooms, and you can introduce them to the software at the same time.

These are only a few of the methods libraries have used to market their virtual reference services to existing customers, and I'm sure you can come up with many others on your own. It is important to remember that your current patrons are a captive audience. You will never find an easier group to advertise to, and you should take every opportunity that presents itself to let them know about your services—virtual and otherwise.

MARKETING TO EVERYONE ELSE

Marketing to existing library users is a relatively cheap and easy way to generate traffic for your new virtual reference service—but it is preaching to the choir. We already have these people. They like us, and we are already doing a pretty good job serving their needs. They will all be happy to hear about your new virtual reference service, and many will be eager to use it, but most of them are already satisfied customers.

The people we most want to persuade of the value of the library and the services we offer are those people who are not currently users. Those who may have used us once, but now get their information from Google or Yahoo or their professor's website; those who buy their books at Amazon.com or Barnes & Noble instead of checking them out from us. Those who need information but are unaware of what the library can do for them, or how convenient it is to get it through our new virtual reference services. There are many benefits for the library if we can demonstrate our value to these potential users. We can expand our market, link the library more closely to the community we serve, and hopefully build a whole new group of library supporters who will be there to back us up when it comes time to ask for money.

But there is one major complication in marketing to new users: they are a much more difficult group to reach. They can be anywhere in the community you serve—in a classroom, on a bus, surfing the Internet, watching television, or walking the dog. In fact, just about the only thing you can really be sure of is that they are not in the library. So how do we get our message out to all these possible audiences?

Advertising for New Users

Libraries are not the first ones to have this problem. Businesses have been struggling with it for years, and when they need to reach a broad audience, their solution is normally to advertise in the mass media—which means television, radio, newspapers, and some sites on the Internet. If you are on a college campus, it means using vehicles like the student newspaper, campus radio station, the university website, and other venues that are viewed by your entire campus population.

As we all know, advertising does not just mean a single ad, it means an entire campaign, with a variety of ads repeated again and again in many different places. In fact, there is a general rule of thumb in advertising that a person must see an ad at least twelve times before they will remember it. Mass marketing is a proven and effective strategy, but it does have one big problem: it costs money . . . lots and lots of money. Money to hire a marketing firm, money to develop the campaign, and money to buy the media. Far more money than most libraries have to spend.

But that doesn't mean we have to give up on mass-market strategies. One possible solution would be to form a cooperative advertising program with other libraries. You are probably familiar with this concept already. It is most commonly found in agricultural marketing cooperatives, where a bunch of small businesses like dairy farmers or raisin growers get together to produce some pretty spectacular advertising like the "Got Milk?" campaign or the famous dancing raisins. Or, if you would like a more literary example, the American Booksellers Association is doing the same thing with its BookSense program to promote independent booksellers.[2] Since many virtual reference services are already based on collaboratives, it would not be hard to ask each member for a small contribution, and together you might be able to come up with a pretty respectable marketing budget. The only difficulty with this approach is that library services are not as interchangeable as milk or raisins. Each library serves its own community in special ways, and it is important that this individuality be maintained in any collaborative marketing venture. If you are already providing a collaborative reference service, that may not be much of a problem. You would probably want some kind of central website similar to the BookSense site, where people could go to log on to your reference service and find out about their local library. However, if each library is providing reference services separately and only marketing collaboratively, the issue may not be so easy to resolve. But that is exactly the kind of problem a good advertising or marketing agency should be able to help you with, and the good news is that if you are working collaboratively, you just might be able to afford it.

Publicity

Advertising is not the only way libraries can get access to the mass media. There is also publicity. Because it is new and novel, virtual reference makes a pretty sexy news story at the moment. It is very easy to get your new service written up in the local newspaper or featured in a segment on television news. Some services like Cleveland's KnowItNow project have even made it onto national news outlets like CNN, National Public Radio (NPR), and the *New York Times*. It doesn't cost you anything to get this attention; all you have to do is send a press release to your local media, cooperate with them to help them write a good story, and then sit back and wait for the calls to roll in. And you had better be prepared for them to roll in. New Jersey's QandANJ service saw its calls increase over 1,000 percent to over 500 calls per day after a story on the service ran in the *Philadelphia Inquirer*—a market that is not even part of their service area. Other services have reported similar results from press coverage in the local media. Press coverage can definitely be an effective strategy for marketing your service to your community, and if you are courting it, you had better be prepared to handle what you get. If you know a story will be coming out, make sure you have backup staff on call to handle the load. The last thing you want to do is have all of those new and eager patrons that you've attracted waiting on hold and eventually hanging up because you are too busy to help them. If people don't have a satisfactory experience the first time they try your service, most of them will not give you another try. So if you are using publicity to market your service, you should be careful what you ask for, because you are likely to get it.

The problem with the "library launches cool new reference service" news coverage most of us get is that it has a limited life span. Traffic will spike for a few days after a story, but it will drop off rapidly after that, as other newer and cooler things compete for your audience's attention. Traffic rarely slides all the way back down to where you were before the story ran, though. After all, you have introduced your service to lots of new potential patrons, and some of them will become regular users. But never as many as you would hope, which means you won't have to worry about keeping that backup staff for long, and it also means that you cannot rely on this kind of opening day publicity as your sole tactic for marketing virtual reference services, as so many libraries have. What you need is a strategy that lets you go back to the media again and again, so that after all of the hoopla surrounding the opening of your service has died down, there is a constant drumbeat of publicity to keep your service fresh in your customers' minds.

There are probably many ways of accomplishing this, but there are two approaches that have proved quite successful for both libraries and bookstores in the past: online programming, and working with the media on a column or other regular feature.

ONLINE PROGRAMS

If your software allows for online meetings, one strategy would be to set up a series of online programs on subjects of interest to your community. These could be chat sessions with authors or other local celebrities, or programs on interesting subjects . . . genealogy, earthquakes, the West Nile virus, how to configure your PC, or how to fill out tax forms. If you're in an academic setting, you could interview professors who are working on interesting research projects, offer a forum on how to do online citations, or even put on an online showcase on MP3 players. You name it, almost any subject will work, as long as there is adequate interest in the community you serve. In many cases, you don't even need to get directly involved in the production of these programs, if you don't want to. There are plenty of people and organizations out there with interesting things to talk about, if you are willing to give them an audience. Of course, each time you have a program, you do a press release to the local media. If you do these often enough, you can create a constant stream of small stories and announcements in the local media that can be just as effective as paid advertising, perhaps more so. Bookstores like Borders and Barnes & Noble have been using this strategy to promote themselves for years now. There is no reason why libraries should not take a page from their book.

COLUMNS AND MEDIA FEATURES

Another approach would be to work with a local newspaper or radio or television station in offering some kind of a regular column or feature program.

A great example of this strategy at work is Mary Dempsey's "Ask a Librarian" segment of NPR's *Rewind* news satire show. Every week the program chooses some interesting or wacky question from a listener and Mary, who is both a librarian and a Chicago Public Library commissioner, answers it on the air.[3] Newspapers and other local media have run similar answer columns and programs for years, sometimes involving librarians and sometimes not. If tracking down the answers to weird questions doesn't suit your fancy, you could always approach one of your area's larger media outlets and offer to provide a "Read More about It" service for their feature stories. The idea would be to do something similar to the "Read More about It" service that came on immediately following certain PBS features and documentaries. It was produced by the Library of Congress and offered selected titles for those who wanted to know more about the subject at hand. You could provide the same service for your local newspaper or television outlets, but include your reference service as a place where people could follow up with questions they might have about the subject matter. If you are in a college or university library, variations of this strategy could be adapted for your campus newspaper and radio station, your alumni magazine, and any other local media programming your campus may already be doing. Remember, too, that these are only a few suggestions; there are dozens of other program ideas that may work as well. Just remember that in order to use the media effectively you need constant exposure. One-off opening day news stories will have little or no lasting effect on your service, any more than running a single ad would. If you truly want to be successful using the media to market your service, you have to find a way to get yourself a "regular gig."

Links from Outside Your Website

Of course, there are other ways to reach new customers in addition to (or instead of) using the mass media. A number of libraries have begun to experiment with adding links to their reference services from outside their library website, such as course websites, department home pages, faculty pages, inside courseware packages like Blackboard and WebCT, and other places potential patrons might be when they need help. MIT's library even managed to get a link to its virtual reference service on the university site's front page for a brief period of time—and got more traffic than it had seen in the entire history of its service. Public libraries could use this strategy by getting their links on pages of the city government's website, or that of the local chamber of commerce (libraries often field business questions referred by the chamber; why not let potential patrons ask right on their site?), as well as community organizations and even schools. The idea here is the same as the "ubiquitous librarian" strategy described previously: don't make your patrons come and find you; take advantage of the capabilities of the virtual reference software to make sure your service is in front of them when they have a question. The problem is that once you start moving off your own website, you are going to have to negotiate with others to give you a presence on their web pages. In many cases, you will also need to find a way to distinguish between questions that should legitimately go to the site that is hosting you, and those that should come to you, but if you can work out the details, the payoff can be substantial.

Ultimately, some have dreamed of carrying this strategy to its final extreme and placing links to library services on Google and other high-traffic search engines, directories, and web resources. However, there are some substantial obstacles to this approach, not the least of which are the fee-based answer services that some search engines—including Google—already offer on their sites. Even if we could find somebody willing to accept us, we'd have to figure out a way to winnow out our patrons from the millions and millions of visitors to those sites. No library—or its funding agency—is ready to take on the information needs of the entire world, even if it were to do so as part of a collective. So I wouldn't expect to see libraries on Google any time soon, and we would probably be better advised to concentrate on our own local strategies rather than wait for a major search engine or web portal to have pity and solve our problems for us.

In this chapter we've reviewed a variety of ideas for marketing your virtual reference service. It is not an exhaustive list by any means, and other opportunities will open up as you go along. That's why in the end, it may not be so important what you do as it is that you do it, and that you take marketing your service every bit as seriously as you do selecting software, developing policies, training staff, or other tasks we all love to spend our time on. While it is possible to have a great virtual reference service with even the most limited software, and it is possible to have a great reference service without policies and without much staff training, you cannot have a reference service at all unless you do what needs to be done to market it and make sure there are people there to use it when you get online.

NOTES

1. For a good overview of this development, see "Web Retailers Try to Get Personal," *New York Times*, 19 August 2002, Technology section.
2. See www.booksense.com.
3. For further details, see an online article in *Newcity Chicago*, at http://www.newcitychicago.com/chicago/lit_50_essay1-00.html.

CHAPTER FIVE

Where Do We Go from Here?

Take a look at the growth of virtual reference over the past three years, and you're reminded of an old Virginia Slims slogan: "You've Come a Long Way, Baby." Just a few years ago, it was tough to find a librarian who even knew what the term meant and fewer still who had ever tried the technology. Today, there are already dozens of articles that have been written on the topic—as you can see from the bibliography at the end of this book—and more are being churned out every week. This is at least the third full-length book to come out on the subject, and I'm sure there are others on the way. We have one conference that is entirely devoted to the subject, and there are "virtual reference tracks" at a number of others. There are more special workshops and seminars on the topic than a person could attend in a lifetime, and it is hard to find a self-respecting library meeting anywhere that does not have at least one program on virtual reference. Of course, all this attention has had its effect, and by now several thousand libraries have "taken the plunge" and decided to offer virtual reference services, either on their own or as part of a growing number of virtual reference collaboratives. While it was once difficult to find a librarian who knew what virtual reference was, today many librarians have been trained on the technology and have had at least some experience working with patrons online. A few of us are even beginning to make a career of it. So it is clear that the exhortations of Anne Lipow and others that we do "in your face reference" have not fallen on deaf ears, and a growing number of libraries are now rushing to join their patrons online.

What is considerably less clear is whether our patrons really care that we're spending all this time, money, and energy to join them on the Web. Despite our arduous efforts to select the best software, train our staff, and make sure we would be ready for our patrons when they came; and despite all the lectures, articles, and just plain hype that have been lavished on the subject for the past few years, the fact of the matter is, most virtual reference services get very little use. If the intent of these services was to enable us to join our users online, so far we have not really accomplished that to any significant extent.

WHERE ARE WE NOW?

The numbers tell the story. Few libraries publish their statistics, but based on data from the 100 virtual reference projects hosted at LSSI, only 10 percent of all virtual reference services currently operating handle more than 300 questions per month. That is less than 10 questions per day, on average. It also represents a very long time between calls for librarians who are tied to their computers waiting for patrons to find them. Of course, some services are busier than others. There are a number that routinely handle 3,000 to 6,000 questions per month, and a few that have handled peak loads of over 500 questions per day. These are impressive statistics, but there's a catch. These heavily used services are invariably large collaborative virtual reference services made up of dozens of individual libraries. In the aggregate, they are handling a lot of traffic, but each separate library is contributing only a few questions to the whole; so, in reality, they are doing no better than the others who are going it alone. In fact, some libraries even report that they are receiving fewer contacts through virtual reference than they were getting in their e-mail reference services, and we know that those were never much to write home about. So even though we librarians have been embracing it with open arms, it's obvious that virtual reference has yet to really catch on among our patrons.

Does this mean that it's time we pulled the plug on virtual reference, packed up our terminals, and headed back to our reference desks—as some have suggested? Although the results so far have not been what many of us expected, it is too early to jump to rash conclusions. It is true that the statistics for virtual reference services are quite low, but most do show a clear upward trend, with some increasing at the rate of 25 percent per quarter or more. Of course, it's not hard to grow at 25 percent per quarter when you're only getting a few hundred questions per quarter to start with. Still, growth is growth, and the trend for most virtual reference services is clearly going in the right direction—in contrast to the continuing decline in the number of questions most of us are seeing at our traditional reference desks.

Also, most libraries have yet to devote any really serious effort to marketing their services. It is very hard to tell how well people will respond to our new virtual reference services when the vast majority of our patrons aren't even aware we offer them. If we librarians can overcome our long-standing aversion to marketing and learn to promote our services more effectively and continuously on the Web and elsewhere, our patrons would at least have a reasonable chance to find out what we have to offer. If they then choose not to use those services, maybe we can feel pretty comfortable about shutting them down. Remember, too, that live online services of all types are still a pretty recent phenomenon. According to a survey conducted by Benchmark Portal, a call-center research center, only 12 percent of all commercial websites offered some form of live, online customer service as of June 2002. Although that number is expected to increase dramatically over the next few years, we are clearly not yet at a point where people expect us to be able to chat with them live and online in the same way as they expect to call us up on the phone, or come down and ask a question at the reference desk.

Another factor that could be limiting the use of our services is the virtual reference technology itself. Much of the software is quite new, and it was originally designed for web collaboration on e-commerce sites, where the content to be shared was relatively limited and easy to control. Virtual reference services place extraordinary demands on this software, and although it has improved greatly over the past few years, it is still far from perfect. It won't work with all computers; there are still some types of web content that cannot be effectively co-browsed without taking extraordinary measures on the patron's computer. Some software packages require that patrons download and install a special plug-in before they can work with a librarian. Many patrons are not used to web collaboration and may find it disconcerting when a librarian "pushes" a page at them. Then there's chat . . . a time-consuming and laborious method of communication, loathed by many librarians and a fair number of our potential patrons as well. So there is little doubt that the tool set we currently have to work with can also discourage the use of our services.

THE NEAR FUTURE

The good news is that things are getting better quickly. The software we are using today is light years ahead of what we had when this was all getting started a few years back. Funds for research and development on the Web are not what they once were, but the technology for web collaboration is getting better all the time. Over the next two to three years, you can expect high-end collaboration software to work with a larger range of computers, operating systems, and network environments, and many of the problems working with proprietary databases and less common forms of web content will be resolved. I also expect that voice will eventually replace chat as the primary method of communicating on these systems, but whether that happens through VoIP or because everyone gets broadband connections or cell phones and frees up their phone lines remains to be seen. You can be relatively sure that the days of chat are numbered, and most of us will not be sorry to see it go. So although the technology may limit access to our virtual reference services for some, it is getting better, and I'm sure that in the long run, web communication and collaboration will be as convenient and easy to use as the telephone is today.

HOW LIBRARIES' COMPETITORS HAVE FARED

Another way to try to get a feel for the future prospects of live reference on the Web is to look at how libraries' would-be competitors are faring. And here we find some decidedly mixed signals.

The Bad News

Most of the original bogeymen we used to fret would put reference librarians out of business—like WebHelp, Ask Jeeves, LookSmart, Answers.com, and dozens of other ask-an-expert and commercial reference sites—went belly-up in the general dot.com collapse, and those few that did manage to survive are barely hanging on in very serious condition. Many of these services did not suffer from lack of use; Ask Jeeves was still getting over 4 million searches per day, even as it was laying off nearly a quarter of its staff. People clearly liked what they had to offer. What killed most of the commercial reference services was not lack of traffic, but lack of a viable economic model. Once Internet advertising dried up and blew away, most had nothing to fall back on, and no choice but to close up shop. Of course, libraries have specialized in giving away things for free for over a century now, so if it is the economic model that was the problem, perhaps we can succeed where they failed. However, it's difficult to imagine any library or group of libraries handling the thousands and thousands of questions these commercial services were getting without a substantial infusion of staff and resources, so perhaps our economic model is not so good after all.

On the other hand, you have "Google Answers." This is a new fee-based reference service which Google launched in April 2002. Customers set their own price on their questions which may range from $2.50 to $200. Questions are answered by an approved group of Google researchers—assuming the price is right. Google retains 25 percent of the question price and the remainder goes to the researcher. The service is not live, it uses web forms, but Google claims that 85 percent of the questions are answered within 24 hours. Although Google Answers is still in the beta stage and is doing little advertising, as of September 2002, it was already averaging over 200 questions per day. Considering that Google gets over 150 million searches per day, one can only imagine what it would get if the company linked Google Answers more directly with the search engine. So here again, we have evidence that people want reference services on the Web, and if Google is able to make a success of the fee-based model, the company will have all the resources it needs to meet the potential demand as the service grows. Compare this to the situation in most libraries, where an increase in demand does not automatically translate into an increase in revenues, and where new patrons must be accommodated within the same static or declining budget. Given our straitened economic circumstances, few librarians would wish Google's success on their worst enemies.

It is also difficult to assess the prospects of the web technologies for live, online customer service that so many libraries are now rushing to adopt. One thing is for certain: it has not caught on nearly as quickly or as widely as many of the software vendors might have wished. The fallout is affecting the entire industry. Three or four years ago during the height of the Internet frenzy, there were probably 50–75 companies peddling live collaboration software, and more and more were jumping into the field every day. Very few of those are still around today, and those that are, are often in desperate financial condition. In fact, it testifies to just how bad things have gotten that some of these companies who once could not have been persuaded to even talk to libraries are now pursuing them as a key market.

As for the experience of e-retailers and other e-commerce sites, it is clear that the technology has not yet been broadly adopted. I've already mentioned the recent Benchmark Portal study showing that less than 12 percent of commercial sites use any kind of real-time collaborative technology. And small wonder. In an article in the *Sydney Morning Herald,* Dave Walker reports on his ill-fated attempts to get customers to use chat on an online loan site, and quotes a 2001 study by Jupiter Research showing that fewer than 4 percent of online buyers say they would take advantage of chat on an e-commerce site.[1] The same study reports that American Greetings, with more than 125,000 subscribers, was reporting no more than a dozen chat sessions per week.

Lands End, one of the earliest and best-known e-commerce sites to use chat, reports somewhat more promising figures. Jaymee Meier, senior customer services manager for Lands End, gave a presentation at a call center conference in 2002 where she indicated that about 8 percent of Lands End's total customer calls are handled by web chat, 17 percent by e-mail, and 76 percent by phone. That's still not a very high percentage, but when you consider that Lands End handles over 15 million calls per year, or about 40,000 to 50,000 calls on a typical day, that translates into an average of 4,200 chats per day, or around 175 sessions per hour—24 hours a day, 364 days a year (they are closed on Christmas). These are statistics any library would be proud to write home about, assuming we could find the staff to answer those questions (Lands End has 180 agents assigned to its chat service). Note, however, that Lands End's e-mail service—something which many libraries have been deemphasizing or abandoning because it did not get enough use—was getting more than twice as much traffic as its chat service—which again leads one to wonder whether we are focusing our attention on the right things in libraries, and whether e-mail reference could have been successful if we had simply promoted it better.

The Good News

It is not all doom and gloom for live interaction technologies. Within the past several years there has been a real boom in instant messaging usage. As of May 2002, Jupiter Communications claimed that there were over 72 million people regularly using one of the major instant messaging services: AOL, MSN, Yahoo, and ICQ. That number was up 17 percent just since November 2001, so use is expanding at a very rapid rate. In fact, Gartner (a well-known technology forecasting firm) predicts that more people will use instant messaging than will use e-mail by 2005.[2] But perhaps more important, instant messaging seems to be evolving from a purely personal technology that allowed people to keep up with their friends and relatives, to a business communications tool that is being used to run online meetings, allow coworkers to stay in touch with one another, and even, yes, chat with customers on company websites. If Gartner is right and this trend continues, it may not be too long before our patrons come to expect to be able to talk live with companies, government, and even libraries over the Web, just as they now expect to be able to reach us by phone and e-mail. This could have a real effect on those anemic virtual reference statistics.

Finally, the fundamentals remain good. People continue to jump on the Web in large numbers despite the dot.com collapse. According to the *Cyberatlas,* more than 54 percent of the total U.S. population was online in September 2001, and that figure appears to be growing at the rate of over 2 million new Internet users each month.[3] Some of the fastest-growing segments are poor and minority users who have not been able to afford web access previously. So the Web is becoming much more democratic and more reflective of the entire society than it once was. People continue to rely on the Web to look for information. The use of Internet search engines is expanding at a rapid rate. Google is now handling more than 150 million searches per day; so in just two days, it handles about the same number of reference questions as all U.S. public and academic libraries combined did in 2001, the most recent year for which data is available. The tools are also improving, and with search engines like Google, natural language searching, linking systems like OpenURL, and other advanced technologies, it is now easier than ever before for people to find the information they need without the assistance of a librarian, or anyone else for that matter. On the other hand, no matter how good the tools get, one suspects that we will never be able to entirely automate the question-answering process, and people will always have real questions and need real answers, not just search results.

THE FUTURE FOR LIBRARIES

It is still a little difficult to evaluate the potential of library reference services on the Web. On the one hand, current virtual reference statistics would seem to indicate that most of our patrons don't know we exist and don't care a fig about all the time, money, and energy we have invested to bring our reference services to them on the Web. But we shouldn't feel too bad, because the evidence also shows that most chat services on commercial websites are not faring much better. On the other hand, the explosion in the use of instant messaging services points to the fact that people like communicating in real time over the Web, at least when they are communicating with their friends, and it is possible that the growth in that technology will also change the way they communicate with commercial websites . . . and even libraries. Finally, we know that people are still flocking to the Web, and that they love to use it to look for information. We also know that they still have questions, and the growth of Google Answers and others indicates that at least some of them are even willing to pay to get their questions answered. So one senses there is some potential for reference services on the Web, if we can find effective ways to let our patrons know they exist, and if we can find effective ways of handling them once they discover us. The question is, how long can we afford to keep these librarians sitting around in front of computers waiting for these services to develop?

Perhaps it is a mistake to focus too narrowly on what is happening—or rather, not happening—on the Web, because while we are waiting for people to find us there, the real immediate potential for virtual reference systems may lie in the way they can help transform the way we do reference with real patrons at real reference desks.

New technologies often get used in ways their developers never imagined. The Internet is a great example; it's highly doubtful that those who designed the original defense communications network ever dreamed that it would one day morph into the online playground/shopping mall/library that it has become. And the situation is the same with virtual reference technologies. Those of us who first began to experiment with virtual reference a few years ago saw it as a way to regain those patrons who had abandoned us for the Web, and to reverse the decline in our traditional reference services. While we know that this solution has met with only limited success, nobody is ready to abandon the web strategy quite yet; some pioneering libraries are beginning to experiment with virtual reference technology to improve the way they deliver information services inside the library.

Other Applications for Virtual Reference Technologies

The same technology that allows us to deliver reference service to patrons on the Web can also be used to deliver service to patrons standing in front of regular reference desks.

FOREIGN-LANGUAGE REFERENCE

The most obvious example of this is foreign-language reference services. Traditionally, if a library wanted to provide reference services in, let's say, Spanish, it meant that the library had to hire bilingual staff and put them behind the reference desk. Good bilingual staff are a relatively scarce commodity, so libraries could normally only afford to provide Spanish-language services in heavily Hispanic areas where they were likely to gets lots of questions—if they could afford to provide such services at all. Spanish-speaking patrons who showed up at other reference desks were just out of luck, or they had to go through the cumbersome and time-consuming process of trying to convey their question to a librarian who did not speak the language, and hoping they could make sense of the answer.

Not so with virtual reference. Virtual reference technologies now allow that same small group of bilingual reference librarians to provide Spanish-language services to many different reference desks at the same time. And that is exactly what the New York Public Library (NYPL) and other public libraries are doing. The NYPL is working on a plan to expand its Spanish-language services from a few branches in the most heavily Hispanic areas to every reference desk in the system, using virtual reference technologies. So when a Spanish-speaking patron comes up to a desk and the librarian cannot understand the question, all the librarian has to do is click on a little icon on her computer screen and the patron is immediately put in touch with a Spanish-speaking librarian who can help the patron find the information they are looking for using the library catalog, the Web, or the library's Spanish-language databases. Because the session is actually taking place at the reference desk, the librarian and the patron can talk over the phone while co-browsing on the Web, and there is no need for cumbersome chat communication that could be difficult for some patrons and many librarians.

ACCESS TO SUBJECT SPECIALISTS

Libraries are using the same model to provide better access to subject specialists at the reference desk. Anyone who has spent any time behind a reference desk knows that there are occasions when we get questions that go beyond our areas of expertise. At such times, you'd really like to have a subject specialist sitting right beside you at the desk that you could turn to for assistance. But no library can afford to staff its desks with subject specialists all the time just to handle an occasional question requiring their expertise, any more than they could afford to staff their desks with polyglot librarians. Usually the best we've been able to do is to refer the question to a subject specialty center if our library or state is lucky enough to have one. This always took extra time, and was inconvenient for most patrons, who would have preferred to have their answer on the spot. But with virtual reference, you can take those same subject specialists and, in effect, put them behind every reference desk in your library. The next time you get a question in law, medicine, business, or some other field that requires special expertise, imagine how nice it would be if all you had to do is click on an icon on the desktop to put the patron in direct contact with an expert at your subject specialty center.

OUTSOURCING

This assumes that your library has access to subject specialty centers, and many libraries do not. Even those that can afford them rarely have all the specialties they want. Here again, virtual reference provides a potential solution. It allows specialty reference centers to deliver services to any library with Internet access, i.e., about 95 percent of the libraries in North America, and a growing percentage of them in the rest of the world. It opens up a market for syndicated reference services that libraries could subscribe to, much as they now subscribe to databases. The operating costs of these subscription services could be distributed over many libraries, so that the cost to each participating library would be much less than it would cost them to develop a subject specialty on their own. It would also allow small and rural libraries that could never afford such services on their own to access them at a price they finally could afford. This is not just conjecture; the James J. Hill Reference Library in St. Paul, Minnesota, one of the best-known business libraries in the country, is developing a business reference service for libraries using virtual reference technology.[4] Subscribing libraries will get their own business website, which is maintained by Hill staff; access to various business databases; online business programming; a document delivery service; and, of course, immediate access to Hill business subject specialists from any reference desk in the library.

If this model proves successful, new and even competing specialty services might develop in a variety of fields including business, law, medicine, statistics, various scientific disciplines, and other areas that have traditionally been difficult for generalists to handle effectively. In the future, it may make more sense for libraries to subscribe to comprehensive subject specialty services, such as Hill's, than it does to subscribe to databases alone—after all, as the Hill slogan goes, "Why just subscribe to a database, when you can get a whole business library at the same price?"

Of course, if you can deliver specialty reference services right to the desk using virtual technology, you can deliver general reference services as well, and some libraries are beginning to do just that. Several state libraries are experimenting with virtual technology to deliver real-time reference services to small rural libraries that have never been able to afford a reference staff of any sort. A number of academic libraries are using virtual reference technology to staff desks at branch and departmental libraries during evenings and weekends when the reference desks would otherwise be closed. The same approach can be used to deliver live reference services to terminals right inside the libraries. In fact, there are already stories about students using virtual reference to contact librarians at reference desks that were just a few feet away rather than give up their seat at the computer; others have used it to report printers that had run out of paper and various other glitches in computer labs that were right inside the building. If you're a student using a catalog up on the fifth floor of the library, virtual reference has to be a lot more attractive than running down and asking a question at the reference desk on the first floor.

THE FUTURE OF THE REFERENCE DESK

Finally, these initiatives raise some very serious questions about the future of the reference desk itself. Let's face it, the reference desk has never been a very good place to do reference. It forces the patron to come and find us when they have a question, rather than having the librarian go find the patron. And very few patrons will take the initiative to find us, either. Reference statistics show that less than 15 percent of patrons who come through the door at academic libraries ever ask a question at the reference desk, and only 20 percent of visitors to public libraries ever come to the desk. There is a large body of literature showing that the reference desk itself can impose substantial barriers to those few who do make it over to ask a question. Some feel the desk can inhibit communication between the patron and the reference staff; it's usually sitting out in the middle of the floor where there is little privacy. Conversation is constrained because everyone is worried about being quiet. What interactions there are sometimes have to be hurried because other patrons may be lined up waiting for help, and on top of all that, the patron is often forced to stand and talk down to a librarian who usually remains comfortably seated. It is certainly not the kind of ambience you would expect for consultations with other professionals like doctors, lawyers, and even accountants, which normally take place in offices with both parties comfortably seated at a desk behind closed doors and away from the prying eyes and ears of other clients. It is hard to imagine that a good consultation with an information professional should require anything less.

The reference desk is also a horribly inefficient place to answer questions. We can only afford to staff it with a few people—generally only one or two are on duty at the same time—which means you can sometimes get long lines, harried librarians, and frustrated patrons when a bunch of people descend on the desk at once. Meanwhile, sometimes hours can go by without a single question. Moreover, we now know from numerous reference studies that the vast majority of questions we get at both public and academic desks really don't require a librarian to handle. Studies show that anywhere from 70 to 85 percent of the questions we get at the reference desk are either directional or requests for known items that can easily be handled by the kind of staff you find at a Barnes & Noble, or by student assistants, with a little training. Yet most of us continue to staff our reference desks at least partially with librarians, just in case somebody does chance to ask a question that requires professional assistance. Finally, because we can't afford to staff our desks with all the possible skills we might need, we sometimes get questions that require subject knowledge or language skills that we can't provide at the desk.

Libraries are not the only ones to have these problems. Banks, airlines, software and hardware companies, the Internal Revenue Service, retailers of all stripes, in fact, virtually any organization that has to answer large numbers of questions from the public has had to deal with exactly the same issues. It wasn't too long ago that most of them dealt with those questions in the same way we handle reference now . . . with thousands and thousands of staff sitting behind desks in local offices all over the country. But not today. In the 1960s, most businesses, government agencies, and others began to close local offices and consolidate their customer inquiry and service operations in large call centers where staff answered questions over the phone instead of sitting behind a desk. And small wonder, because consolidating staff in call centers can significantly improve the efficiency of any customer interaction that can be handled over the phone. Centralized staff operate more efficiently, which means that it takes fewer librarians to answer the same number of questions when the librarians are all sitting in a call center than it does if they are each sitting behind a separate desk. Staff in call centers can also be tiered so that routine questions can be routed to front-line customer service staff, while those that require more expert assistance can be directly routed to professional staff or subject specialists. It is a highly efficient operation, and it can greatly reduce the cost of handling customer interactions of all types. For example, a typical bank transaction costs $22.50 to handle if the customer comes into a branch, but only $1.14 if the same transaction is handled over the phone. So it should come as no surprise that, according to Ron Zemke in the *Harvard Business Review,* by 1996 over 70 percent of all customer interaction was taking place in call centers. And these call centers are handling everything from the simplest catalog orders to complex technical support, engineering, and even medical issues.

Reference service is the exception. While the rest of the world has moved its question-answering operations into call centers, libraries have continued to do reference much as they always have—with thousands and thousands of librarians sitting behind reference desks. To be fair, reference did not easily lend itself to the telephone. Much of the material needed to answer reference questions was in books in the library collection, and unless it was a question of a brief factual nature—something the librarian could easily look up and read—it was pretty difficult to share much of that material over the phone. But this is no longer true. Today, much of the material we use to answer reference questions is online . . . and many of our patrons prefer the convenience of electronic access even when a book might be the better source. But most important, virtual reference allows librarians and patrons to work together online much more effectively than they ever could over the phone. We may finally have the tools we need to get librarians out from behind the reference desk and to rationalize the entire reference process, much as our commercial cousins have been using the telephone and call center technology to restructure their customer service operations over the past forty years.

It is too early to tell exactly how this might work, but some libraries are already beginning to experiment with the concept. The King County Library System (KCLS) outside of Seattle is busy developing a centralized reference center that will initially handle all telephone and web reference services for the system's forty-two branches. If this proves successful, KCLS then plans to see how it might take advantage of the centralized reference staff to change the way branches are staffed. The long-range objective is to develop a system that will both let the staff reach out to patrons on the Web and enable them to handle the questions they are already getting in a more efficient and effective manner. In academic libraries, the need to find ways to restructure reference services is even more immediate and profound. When you see your reference statistics declining 50 percent or more over a period of five years, as is commonly the case in academic libraries now, the cost of answering those questions continues to rise, and it is becoming increasingly difficult to justify continuing to do business as we always have.

I know there are many of you who consider call centers and centralized reference services an anathema, and some of you would never consider getting rid of your reference desks, even if you could only afford to staff them a few hours a week. But I would caution you not to dismiss these possibilities too lightly. One of the important advantages of call center technology is that it has allowed companies the flexibility to outsource their customer service operations to businesses that specialize in this area and can answer questions more efficiently and effectively and at less cost than the company can itself. In fact, today when you call an airline, a catalog retailer, a cable company, or your PC technical support line, there is a very good chance you are talking with an employee of one of these outsourcers, rather than a representative of the company itself. Of course, that makes no difference to us, as long as we get our question answered right—in fact, in most cases, we aren't even aware that our questions are being answered by another company.

This is both the danger and the promise of virtual reference. Because it is quite possible that we librarians who are still sitting behind reference desks are a lot like the staff that used to sit behind thousands of customer service desks and counters back before the telephone and call center technologies came along and changed their jobs forever. Virtual reference could play a similar transformative role at the reference desk. If it can be proven that these new technologies can significantly reduce the cost of reference services, and if our patrons take to them as willingly as they have taken to customer service over the phone, then the days of our traditional desk reference services could certainly be numbered. If we librarians remain unwilling to explore these options, and to rethink reference from the ground up, I can assure you there are others waiting in the wings who are ready to use these new technologies to reinvent our libraries for us. The irony is that the very same virtual reference technologies we have so eagerly embraced to try and reach our patrons on the Web might someday be used to displace us at the reference desk.

THE CRYSTAL BALL

There are a lot of "ifs" in that last paragraph . . . just as there have been a lot of "ifs" throughout this book. That is because we are just beginning to experiment with this new technology, and there seem to be so many possibilities and so much we do not know. What type of collaboration will prove most effective for doing reference on the Web? Will voice over IP come into its own, or will our patrons prefer to communicate using chat or instant messaging? How many sessions can a librarian handle at once? And what makes a good virtual reference librarian, anyway? And how should we train and evaluate them? Can libraries be successful in marketing these services, and if so, how? And where is all this leading us in the end? Is virtual reference just another "technology fad" like e-books or Z39.50 searching that will grab our attention briefly and then fizzle out after a few years, or is something more fundamental afoot here? Will virtual reference really allow us to join our patrons on the Web, and will our patrons really care if we do? What happens if it really does take off? How will we ever staff it? How can we ever scale up our services to meet the potential demands of the Web? And finally, what effect will these new technologies have on our traditional services, and what is likely to become of those of us who are working behind those reference desks? Throughout this book, we've speculated and conjectured on these and other issues and looked at how some libraries are trying to answer them. But the truth of the matter is, nobody knows the answers to any of these questions for certain. Virtual reference is a brand new field, and we are all making it up as we go along. The only thing of which we can be relatively certain is that we have let the genie of virtual reference out of the bottle. And now we should be very careful what we wish for, because we just might get it.

NOTES

1. Dave Walker, "Mum's the Word for the Chattering Classes," *Sydney Morning Herald,* 23 October 2001.
2. "Instant Messaging Highlights Unpredictability of Business Technologies," *Boston Globe,* 25 March 2002.
3. "U.S. Internet Population Continues to Grow," *Cyberatlas,* 6 February 2002, at www.cyberatlas.internet.com.
4. See http://www.jjhill.org/vrtoolkit/index.html.

APPENDIX A

SOFTWARE FEATURE CHECKLIST

This appendix contains a comprehensive list of features and characteristics that are available on one or more of the software packages that libraries are using for virtual reference services. No one package offers all of these features, nor are you likely to find any one application that has absolutely everything you want. So a good way to start the software selection process is to review the list of features available, select all of those you would like to have, and then rank them according to their importance to you. Give the feature a 1 if you feel it is something you just can't do without, a 2 if the feature is important but not absolutely critical, and a 3 or higher if it would be nice to have, but you could live without out it. Rank the features of each of the packages you are considering seriously and then compare costs, company reliability, and other purely business issues, such as whether the software is already being used by other libraries with whom you might want to collaborate. Your rankings should help you identify which features you can give up without compromising the core functionality you want, or, if you do have to compromise on core features, at least you will know exactly what you are losing.

Different types of software features and characteristics are treated in the following sections of this appendix:

1. Patron Requirements
2. Engaging the Patron
3. Patron Authentication
4. Communication
5. Content Sharing
6. Database Co-browsing
7. Session Transcripts
8. Patron Profiling

9. Online Meetings
10. Satisfaction Surveys
11. Librarian's Interface
12. Librarian Training, Support, and Documentation
13. Administration
14. Licensed or Hosted
15. Queuing and Routing Structure
16. Customization

1. PATRON REQUIREMENTS

One of the most important characteristics of any virtual reference software is what the patron is required to do to access the software. Ideally, you want a system that puts as few barriers between the patron and the librarian as possible. And one of the most common barriers is patron downloads—software packages that require patrons to download, install, or configure something on their computers before they can use your service. E-commerce sites, web customer service companies, and most libraries that work with the general public have usually tried to avoid patron downloads because they can create significant barriers for many patrons. However, some of the most sophisticated software features such as voice over IP and videoconferencing usually require patron downloads, and a few libraries—particularly academic libraries where students and faculty may already be downloading other software—are experimenting with software that requires downloads in an effort to take advantage of some of these advanced capabilities. These experiments are still in the very early stages yet, and it is too early to tell whether software downloads will be a serious barrier in the academic reference environment or not.

Also, bear in mind that not all downloads are equally problematic. Clearly the worst kind are proprietary downloads, where the patron must download and install a special program just to work with your virtual reference service. And even within proprietary downloads there are differences; some are small and download and install automatically, while others are large, or require the patron to go through a complete installation and configuration process. Obviously, the more you require the patron to do, the less likely they are to cooperate with you, and the more likely they are to encounter problems if they do.

Then there are some software applications that require RealAudio, Macromedia Flash, or some other web utility. These tend to be less of a problem because they are already in use in many web applications, and so there is a good chance that your patrons may already have them downloaded and installed. Moreover, software companies like RealAudio and Macromedia Flash spend millions of dollars to make sure that their applications will download and work easily with many different types of computers and operating systems, so their products generally present fewer problems than some proprietary downloads that may not have been tested in every conceivable environment.

Finally, there are the instant messaging programs like those offered by AOL, MSN, and Yahoo. Each of these also requires a patron download, but there is a good chance that at least some of your patrons already have it—this is particularly true if you are in an academic environment, or working with a younger patron population. And here again, these companies work hard to make sure their software downloads easily and works on as many different types of machines as possible.

However, downloads are not the only element that can affect whether patrons can access your service or not. Many virtual software applications will only work on PCs, or with certain operating systems or certain types or versions of browsers. Others require a certain minimum speed for the patron's Internet connection, while others won't work if the patron is behind a firewall, and so on. Even when the software truly is cross-platform compatible, you will often find that some (usually critical) features may not be supported on all operating systems. It is impossible here to list every potential condition that might limit access to your service from the patron side. But in reviewing the various software packages, it is important that you carefully study exactly what the patron needs to do to access the software, and how the software works or does not work with various types of computers, operating systems, browsers, network environments, and Internet connections.

Finally, you will want to give some consideration as to how well the software works with screen readers and other adaptive software. This is a relatively new area of concern for many of the companies developing interactive software, as it is to many libraries, and so you will find that many programs do not yet work correctly with all adaptive software. However, this situation is improving as companies work to address the issue. Also keep in mind that for many persons with disabilities—particularly those with mobility or hearing impairments—virtual reference software may be the most effective way for them to gain access to your reference services.

Patron Requirements	Y/N	Rank	Comments
Download required on patron side?			
If so, what type?			
Proprietary to software			
Size			
Installation or configuration required			
Standard utility (RealAudio, Flash, other)			
Instant messaging			
Patron operating system requirements			
Patron browser requirements			
Patron connection requirements			
Patron firewall or network requirements			
System works with adaptive software and devices?			

2. ENGAGING THE PATRON

"Engaging the patron" refers to how patrons access the software. In almost all cases, the patron clicks on some sort of link, icon, or button to connect with the librarian. However, where that link is, what it looks like, and how much control the library has over it can vary greatly between software packages. Some software applications insist you use their own icon or logo on your web page, while others allow you to completely customize it for your library so that nobody knows what the underlying application is. Although in most cases, the link to reference service is accessed from the library website, a few packages allow patrons to download a link to the service so it can be accessed right on their browser toolbar whenever they are on a domain the library has registered; others have special icons patrons can download and place on their desktops so they can reach you with a single click any time they have a question. The only complication here is that the ability to put an icon on the patron's desktop or browser usually requires some sort of download on the patron's side, so keep that limitation in mind when considering this feature. Another feature available in some programs is a "proactive" link that allows you to watch patrons on your website and automatically initiate a session when someone looks like they need help. Although a few libraries have tried this strategy, most have shied away from it because of the obvious privacy concerns.

Engaging the Patron	Y/N	Rank	Comments
How does patron access system?			
Icon or link on library website			
Icon or link on patron's browser			
Icon or link on patron's desktop			
Link or icon fully customizable for library?			
Proactive link, librarian can initiate session with patron			

3. PATRON AUTHENTICATION

Most libraries using virtual reference systems want some way to authenticate patrons coming on to the system. (Note: This is a separate issue from authenticating patrons in your proprietary databases, which is addressed under "Database Co-browsing" below.) Libraries have used a variety of authentication strategies, ranging from very weak approaches like having the user enter their zip code to very stringent ones, such as requiring that each user have a "certificate" before they are able to access your reference services. One method that has not yet been adopted by libraries, but could be, is a registry, where users register once on the system (like Amazon.com) and then do not have to identify themselves anew every time they come back.

The important point in evaluating virtual reference packages is to determine whether the software will support the authentication system you want to use (not all will support certificates, for example) and if so, whether the authentication piece is built in to the software, or it is something you or your IT department will have to add on yourself.

Patron Authentication	Y/N	Rank	Comments
Built in to software?			
What types supported (zip code, library card, registry, etc.)?			
Have to build it yourself			
Will software work with your existing authentication methods?			

4. COMMUNICATION

This section covers the various methods of communication between the librarian and the patron. Of course, the default method for almost all packages currently on the market is chat or some form of typing messages back and forth. But all chat is not alike. Some programs—particularly the instant messaging software—allow you to include little smiley faces or "emoticons" with your chat; others offer a spelling-check function on chat, a nice feature for those of us who have always been a little challenged in that department; and still others allow you to block certain words and phrases so you can restrict what particularly nasty patrons can say to you.

Voice communications are also an option . . . and an option many librarians would definitely prefer over chat, which can be a time-consuming and cumbersome way to handle a reference session. Technically, almost any software package on the market has voice capacities, because the librarian can always call the patron up and talk over the phone while they use the software to interact with the patron on the Web. Of course, this assumes the patron has a free phone line, but that's not much of a stretch if you are working in an academic environment where the students and faculty are often on network connections. And it is becoming increasingly likely for the rest of us as well, as DSL, cable modems, and cell phones become more common.

But if you want voice communication and the patron does not have another line, then you will need some sort of web-based voice communication. The primary options here are VoIP (voice over Internet Protocol) and streaming audio. Voice over IP may be simplex—like a CB radio, where only one person can talk at a time—or duplex, like a telephone, where both parties can talk at once. Voice over IP is still pretty much a frontier technology. It usually requires a high-speed connection to use it effectively, and although many computers may be capable of handling it, many patrons will not know how to configure their computers to take advantage of it. So if you are considering VoIP, check carefully for the requirements on the patron side. It is also nice if the package comes with a "wizard" or some sort of automated program that helps the patron configure their computer to use this feature. Also, be aware that VoIP usually requires a download on the patron side, but most programs will "fall back" to chat if the patron does not want to download, or their computer simply cannot support this feature.

If you still want to use audio, but don't want to go as far as VoIP, think about streaming audio. This software is commonly used to broadcast music, news, and other web programs, and it works well for one-way voice from the librarian to the patron, and for classroom situations where a teacher is speaking to a class. But it is not designed for two-way real time communication in reference sessions, and it also requires that patrons download and configure RealAudio, Apple QuikTime, or similar applications.

Getting video over the Internet is much like audio . . . except the requirements are even more stringent. Of course, you need to have a camera, and the appropriate software on both the patron's and librarian's computers, and you need a high-speed network connection if you want to see anything other than a jerky, freeze-frame version of the person on the other end of the call. However, if you are still interested in either audio or video and you don't want to wait for it to get easier or better, you can easily test it out right now, because several instant messaging programs now include both VoIP and video, and these features are available completely free of charge.

Finally, there are a few specialized features that may be of particular use in virtual reference systems. First, does the software have some kind of "back channel" feature that allows reference staff to contact each other while they are online? This feature can be very helpful when you have a number of librarians logged on to the software who are not in the same physical location. Second, how well does the software integrate e-mail and other reference service points? Many questions cannot be answered completely in a live session, and the librarian has to follow up with the patron later on—usually via e-mail. Likewise, there are patrons who contact us first via e-mail, or at the desk or by phone, and it would be great if there were a single application that would help keep track of all our reference activity regardless of what venue the patron chooses to use. At this point, there are some virtual reference applications that integrate chat and e-mail . . . but none yet that truly cover all service points. Finally, how well does the software communicate with other virtual reference services and other libraries? This is still a very fluid area, but as virtual reference becomes more popular, librarians may want to transfer patrons to other virtual reference services, or to evolving reference networks like the Collaborative Digital Reference Service. There are no standards in this area as yet, but some are under development, so this is an area to keep your eyes on.

Communication	Y/N	Rank	Comments
Chat			
Spell check			
Emoticons			
Language blocking			
Multilingual support			
VoIP (voice over Internet protocol)			
Simplex (one-way)			
Duplex (two-way)			
Streaming audio			
Patron set-up wizard			
Connection requirements			
Hardware requirements			
Software requirements			
Video			
Interactive (two-way video)			
Streaming video			
Patron set-up wizard			
Connection requirements			
Hardware requirements			
Software requirements			

Communication	Y/N	Rank	Comments
Back channel for staff			
E-mail integration			
Phone and desk reference integration			
Standards support / communication with other systems			

5. CONTENT SHARING

Information sharing is what reference is all about, and the true measure of any virtual reference software lies in the range of different types of content it allows you to share and the level of interaction it permits you to have with your patrons. The rule of thumb in this area is the more the better—with one major qualification. Some of the most advanced forms of collaboration, such as application sharing and the ability to mark up the patron's screen, either require a download on the patron's side or only work with certain operating systems and browsers, so, in evaluating these various collaborative features, be sure to pay particular attention to any special requirements on the patron's side.

The collaborative features most commonly found in virtual reference software include the following ones.

Screenshots. The ability to send a screenshot of a window or other area of the librarian's desktop to the patron can be a great help. The screenshot is just a picture, so none of the links work, but it does display the content. This is a very useful feature for sharing proprietary databases and other content that you cannot co-browse with the patron. In some low-end software, this is the only method of sharing web pages with the patron; in higher-end programs, it is a useful supplementary feature when other co-browsing techniques don't work.

Automated screenshots. Some programs allow you to send automated screenshots, so that a new image of a window is sent to the patron every ten or fifteen seconds or at some interval specified by the librarian. Again, these are just pictures, but it could be a useful feature when the librarian is trying to show the patron a process—like how to search a database—and does not want to have to manually send an individual screenshot at each step along the way.

Slide shows. A number of software packages allow you to share slide shows with the patron. In some cases the slide shows may need to be in a special format, but in others PowerPoint or other standard packages may be used. Some software allows you to associate a script that goes out automatically with each slide. Some programs allow you to run the shows automatically; others must be displayed manually by the librarian. This is a very useful feature for online instruction and training, and for online programming.

File sharing. Many programs permit you to send files to the patron, and in some cases these will open directly in the patron's browser. This can be a very useful feature for sharing copies of articles and other content in text or Adobe Acrobat formats, and many libraries also use this feature to send scanned images of books from their regular collections.

Page pushing. This is the ability to send a live web page to the patron—in contrast to the static screenshots described above. In some programs, each web page opens up in a separate window on the patron's computer, which can be a bit confusing if you are sharing a lot of web pages. In other cases, the web pages open up right in the patron's browser, with each new page replacing the previous one.

Co-browsing. This is sometimes called collaborative browsing, "follow-me" browsing, or "escorting," and it is a feature of the higher-end software applications. It allows the librarian to take control of the patron's browser and escort them around the Web, so that everywhere the librarian goes, the patron follows along automatically. With some programs, this feature is two-way, so that either the librarian or the patron may do the driving—which is useful if the patron wants to show the librarian where they were having problems with a search. A few programs allow the librarian to shift control of the session to allow the patron to lead, and then to take back control when desired. It is also important that the librarian be able to disable co-browsing when necessary, because you don't necessarily want the patron to follow you down those blind alleys you sometimes have to explore to find the answers to some reference questions.

Form sharing. This is the ability to share text in search boxes or other text fields on web pages. It is very useful for demonstrating how to develop effective search strategies on the Web. This is also a two-way feature in some systems, so the text the patron enters also shows up on the librarian's side, and you can do collaborative search-strategy development.

Interacting with patron's screen. Some of the more advanced programs allow you to interact with the patron's screen. In addition to pushing content, you may be able to scroll their screen, highlight particular links, or even draw or mark up their screen. In some cases, you may even be able to see both the librarian's mouse and the patron's mouse on the screen at the same time. Some of these features may require a patron download, so pay particular attention to patron requirements with these applications.

White board. This feature allows patrons and librarians to draw, type, paint, and scribble together on a shared online white board. This feature normally requires a download on the patron side, but it can be quite useful for homework help and other applications where you want to share more than web pages and text content.

Application sharing. This is one of the most advanced collaborative features available in virtual reference software, in that it allows the librarian to actually take over and operate the patron's computer remotely. It allows the librarian to remotely operate not only the patron's browser, but also any other software on their machine. Application sharing solves many of the difficulties with database co-browsing, authentication, and other issues that arise with other collaborative technologies. But there are also a couple of big catches with application sharing. First, it always involves a download on the patron's side, and second, application sharing can raise serious security issues with patrons, because librarians can do anything they want—including format the hard drive—once they gain access to the patron's machine. We know that there are very few librarians who would intentionally mess up a patron's computer, but some patrons may be a little more difficult to convince. Another issue is speed. Since the entire content of the patron's computer must be fed back to the librarian, application sharing usually requires a lot more bandwidth to work effectively than comparable programs without this feature. So despite its obvious utility, up until now most libraries have steered clear of application sharing, because of the download requirement and the security concerns.

Finally, no software is perfect, so when evaluating software, be sure to ask what types of content cannot be co-browsed and what sort of workarounds are available in such cases.

Content Sharing	Y/N	Rank	Comments
Screenshots			
Automated screenshots			
Slideshows			
What slide formats			
Script goes with slides			
Slideshows can be automated			
File sharing			
What types?			
Will open in patron's browser			
Page pushing			
Opens separate window			
Opens in same browser			
Co-browsing			
One-way			
Two-way			
Collaboration can be stopped at will			
Librarian may choose who will lead			

Content Sharing	Y/N	Rank	Comments
Form sharing			
One-way			
Two-way			
Interacting with patron's screen			
Scrolling page			
Highlighting links			
Drawing on patron's screen			
Ability to see each other's cursor			
White board			
Special features (math equations, etc.)			
Application sharing			
What types of applications may be shared?			
How are security concerns handled?			
What sort of connection is recommended?			
What types of content cannot be shared with the patron?			

6. DATABASE CO-BROWSING

Co-browsing databases presents a special problem for virtual reference software because none of the packages currently on the market were originally designed with that function in mind. Although a variety of different technologies have been developed to try to address this problem, none of them works perfectly, and there are advantages and disadvantages to each. Moreover, how well a particular co-browsing technology works for you has a lot to do with how you mount your databases (locally mounted or accessed through a vendor's website), how you authenticate patrons, and even the type of network your library is on. So you should use this section as a general guide for identifying the types of technologies and software that may work best for you . . . but if co-browsing databases is important to you, then there is no substitute for actually testing the software in your own environment with your own databases.

That said, there are three basic co-browsing technologies used in virtual reference software (some of the software packages actually make use of several), and patron requirements will vary according to the technology used. So as you are evaluating packages, make sure you understand both the type (or types) of co-browsing offered, and what the patron requirements are for each type.

URL-pushing co-browsing. This is basic co-browsing technology offered by the majority of virtual reference software currently on the market. It works on a very simple model whereby the librarian's browser sends instructions to the patron's browser to go to a particular URL, so both the librarian and the patron are visiting the site independently. You can think of this model as an H where one leg of the H is the patron's browser, the other is the librarian's browser . . . and the crossbar is the connection between them. Although it will work with some databases, URL-pushing technology is normally the least effective type in database co-browsing because it will not work with the IP authentication schemes used by many libraries (the librarian is authenticated, the patron's computer is not), and because it is difficult to coordinate two computers inside many databases. If you want to see a good example of the problems, try co-browsing the PubMed database at www.pubmed.gov with any software that uses URL-pushing technology. There are no authentication issues here because PubMed is a freely accessible database. However, you will find that the patron and librarian will lose collaboration in the brief results list, but regain it when the librarian clicks on a full record. That is just one example of the many problems you can run into trying to co-browse databases using the URL-pushing strategy.

Proxy server co-browsing. This is a more advanced technology found in a few of the more sophisticated virtual reference packages. In proxy server co-browsing, both the patron and the librarian are connected to another computer, called a "proxy server," that actually does the browsing and feeds the content back to both the patron's and the librarian's browsers. You can imagine that proxy server co-browsing looks like a Y with the tail of the Y representing the proxy server that is doing the browsing, and the two arms of the Y the content being fed back to both the librarian and the patron.

Proxy server co-browsing has several advantages. First, because a single computer with a known IP address is doing the browsing, proxy server co-browsing will accommodate IP authentication, although it may require some special software and configuration to make it work effectively. Second, and most important, because there is only one computer doing the browsing, you don't have the same problems trying to synchronize the librarian's and patron's browsers.

As a result, proxy server technology allows you to co-browse a much larger number of proprietary databases than is possible with the URL-pushing approach. Although the proxy server approach works much better in databases than URL pushing, it is not perfect. In the first place, not all proxy servers are alike; some work much more reliably and with a much larger number of databases than others, so make sure you actually try the technology out on your databases, and don't just take someone's word for what they can do. Second, no matter how good the proxy server, there are still databases that even the best of them won't be able to handle. So you'll want to know which databases can't be co-browsed, and what sort of work-arounds are available to handle these exceptions. Finally, you can sometimes run into graphics display problems in some proprietary databases when using proxy server co-browsing. This is because some proxy servers have the librarian's and patron's computers request the website graphics separately rather than sending them through the proxy server to save time, but the database refuses the request because it does not recognize either the patron or the librarian as an authenticated user . . . because only the proxy server has been authenticated. To avoid this problem, you need to use a proxy server with "image funneling," meaning that all graphics requests from authenticated sources must be funneled through the proxy server, and you should not have any problem with image display.

Application sharing. The third database co-browsing strategy is the application-sharing technology described in the "Content Sharing" section above. With application sharing, the librarian simply takes control of the patron's computer and operates it remotely. It works better than any other approach for co-browsing proprietary databases, because the databases just see the requests as coming from the patron's browser. So application sharing allows you to do just about anything and go just about anywhere the patron can go on the Web. In theory it works wonderfully, but there are several major drawbacks to the application-sharing technology. First, it always requires a download on the patron's side. Second, application sharing may raise significant security concerns with some patrons. And third, application sharing requires a fairly robust Internet connection to work effectively, because all the graphic content and other program information must be piped over the Internet to the librarian's computer, and it is almost impossible to do that effectively with a standard dial-up connection.

Database Co-browsing	Y/N	Rank	Comments
Co-browsing technologies available			
URL pushing			
Proxy server			
Application sharing			
Database authentication strategies			
User name / password			
IP authentication			
Special software required			
Works with authentication software used by your institution			
What databases can't be co-browsed			
Work-arounds for databases and content that can't be co-browsed			

7. SESSION TRANSCRIPTS

Many of the more sophisticated virtual reference systems can produce and store detailed transcripts of reference sessions. Patrons like the transcripts because they give them something to refer back to after they log off, and libraries are finding that transcripts provide new and effective methods for understanding and evaluating what goes on in the reference process. In fact, there are currently a number of major academic research initiatives under way to examine reference transcripts in order to get a better picture of what really goes on in virtual reference sessions.

However, like so much else in virtual reference, all transcripts are not created equal. Here are some of the features you will want to keep in mind when selecting a virtual reference application.

Integrated verbatim transcripts. Some systems produce integrated verbatim transcripts, which include all chat and the URLs of web pages browsed or other content shared in an integrated format. Others produce transcripts that separate chat from the URLs, and others show only chat or only URLs. Integrated transcripts are preferable because they allow patrons and others to easily read through a transcript and see exactly what happened and in what order. It is also helpful if the transcripts contain live links, so all you need to do is click to bring up the web page or other content.

E-mail and storage. Many systems will automatically e-mail a copy of the transcript to the patron, the librarian, and other parties. If the system does e-mail transcripts, check to see if the e-mails can be customized for your library by adding boilerplate material such as contact information and other details. Systems that produce transcripts usually store the data in a database where it can be accessed later. If transcripts are stored, it is also useful to have a good search feature so they can be easily found and retrieved from the database later; some systems only allow you to access them by session number or by patron ID.

Who owns the data? Often both the software and the transcript database are hosted on the vendor's servers. If this is the case, make sure you understand just who owns the data (you or the vendor), and just how much control you have over it. Regardless of who owns it, you will want to know how long it is archived, when and how it can be deleted, and what happens in case of disputes, subpoenas, warrants, and other legal actions. If you are concerned about security issues, you will also want to know what steps have been taken to protect the data regardless of whether it is housed on your machines or on the vendor's.

Analytical tools. What sorts of tools are available for analyzing the transcripts? Virtual reference systems can produce thousands of transcripts, and you will need all of the analytical tools you can get to help you make sense of them. Examples include word frequency analysis tools, timestamps on chat during sessions so you can measure lags in conversation, and benchmark data so you can compare the performance of your service with others.

Transcripts	Y/N	Rank	Comments
Session transcripts available?			
Verbatim			
Live links			
How retrieved? Session number, by patron ID, search engine?			
Transcripts can be e-mailed?			
Automatic			
Who gets them: patron, librarian, others?			
Content of e-mail can be customized?			

Transcripts	Y/N	Rank	Comments
Data protection			
Who owns data?			
How much control do you have over it?			
Data security measures			
Analytical tools			

8. PATRON PROFILING

"Patron profiling" means that the software collects and stores data on patrons and how they use your reference service. These patron profiles are keyed to the patron's name, e-mail address, or some other identifying feature, and they generally provide information on the patron's previous visits to your service, the questions they asked, who served them, and so on. Patron profiles typically pop up automatically when the patron logs on or can be easily accessed during a session so the librarians can review the information. Profiling is an important feature in the commercial world—where many of these packages were developed—because the more a business knows about its customers, the easier it is to tailor products and services to meet their needs. This is also true of reference services, because the more we know about the way a patron uses our services and the types of interests they have, the easier it is for us to provide services that meet their specific needs—and this is particularly true in large, distributed reference services, where a patron may never deal with the same librarian twice. However, profiling systems also raise major privacy issues for libraries, because there are occasions when patrons may not want to have their questions and interests tracked and recorded.

Most virtual reference systems that store session transcripts also offer patron profiling, so in evaluating these systems, you'll want to know not only the kind of data that is collected and stored in the patron profile, and how it is accessed within the system, but also whether patrons are allowed to opt out of the profiling and remain anonymous on the system. Or you may want the ability to set "anonymity" as the default option and only profile patrons who have expressly requested it. You may even want the ability to disable the profiling system altogether. As with session transcripts, you will also want to know who owns the data, where it is stored, who has access to it, how much control you have over it, and how well it is protected.

Patron Profiling	**Y/N**	**Rank**	**Comments**
Patron profiling available?			
What data is collected in profile?			
How are profiles accessed?			
Privacy protection			
Patrons allowed to opt out?			
Default anonymity—patrons must opt in?			
Profiling system may be disabled?			
Data protection			
Who owns data?			
How much control do you have over it?			
Data security measures			

9. ONLINE MEETINGS

Although virtual reference software was primarily designed for one-on-one reference sessions between a single librarian and a patron, some systems also allow you to have online meetings where many people may be on a session at the same time. This feature can be very useful for online bibliographic instruction and classes of all types, as well as online programming. If the software offers this feature, you will want to know if the software functions the same way in online meetings as in regular reference sessions (some software offers a more limited set of features in online meetings than in regular reference sessions). You will also want to know the maximum number of people the software will support on a meeting, whether you can have multiple librarians on a meeting, and whether the content of the meeting can be archived so that it can be posted and accessed later. Finally, some software packages offer special meeting management features that allow you to better control sessions with large numbers of participants. These features might include the ability to block chat from the audience when the librarian or instructor is speaking; giving participants the ability to raise their hand and be recognized when they have a question; the ability to remove an individual from a meeting; and other features that allow you better control over the session.

Online Meetings	Y/N	Rank	Comments
Online meetings available?			
Maximum number of participants			
Multiple librarians allowed?			
Any software features not available in meetings?			
Meeting archives available?			
Meeting management features?			

10. SATISFACTION SURVEYS

Some virtual software applications offer satisfaction surveys that may be automatically sent to patrons or librarians or both at the completion of a reference session. If this feature is available, you will want to know whether the survey can be customized for your library (it is also useful if there is a good default survey available that you can modify if necessary), whether it can be sent to both the librarian and the patron, whether the survey can be linked with the actual session transcript, and what kind of reporting and analysis tools are available to help you analyze the data.

Satisfaction Surveys	Y/N	Rank	Comments
Satisfaction surveys available?			
Sent to patrons			
Sent to librarians			
May be customized for library?			
Default survey available?			
Linked to session transcript			
Reporting and analysis tools available?			

11. LIBRARIAN'S INTERFACE

All virtual reference software has two sides: the patron interface and the interface the librarians and reference staff use to work with the patrons. In some cases, as in free instant messaging programs, these interfaces look exactly the same and both patrons and librarian have the same set of tools. However, in most commercially available virtual reference software, the librarian uses a special interface with tools and features not found on the patron side. Systems differ substantially in the kinds of tools and features they offer, and new ones keep coming out all the time. However, here is a list of the most commonly available features as of this writing; just keep your eyes open for new tools as you are evaluating packages.

Ability to work with multiple patrons. Perhaps the most critical feature on the librarian's side is the ability to deal with more than one patron at a time. Virtual reference is well suited for multiple sessions because you can take a patron to a particular website and get them started, while you go off and work with another patron. This can save a lot of staff time in busy reference services, but the software must be able to support multiple sessions effectively in order for it to work. In general, this means having an interface that is designed for working with multiple questions, making it easy to switch from one patron to another, timing the activity in each session so you can see how long it's been since you've heard from that patron, and so on. Ask the vendor for details on its multiple patron support, and try it out, if possible, in real-life situations to see how well it actually works.

Scripts. These are canned text messages used to avoid retyping commonly used expressions, like "I think I've found something that might help answer your question, can I send it to you?" or "Does this completely answer your question?" and others. Most librarians find scripts very helpful. Look for software that makes them as easy to add, delete, and modify as possible. Also look for software that makes it easy for each staff member to have his or her own scripts and to share a group of them with other librarians on the system. Finally, it is very nice if the system comes with a default set of scripts that have been tested for reference needs, so you don't have to invent them from scratch when you are first getting started.

Bookmarks. Similar to scripts, bookmarks help you quickly get to places on the Web. Again, you are looking for flexibility in adding, modifying, and deleting bookmarks, and for the ability to have your own personal set, as well as a set you share with others. Because it is possible to have many bookmarks, you should also be looking for systems that allow you to organize and categorize your bookmarks to make them easier to find while in a session.

Audio and visual alerts. Some software packages provide you with audio or visual alerts (ding, ring, flash, etc.) when a patron comes on or when the patron sends through a new chat message. These alerts can be quite useful for those of us who are easily distracted when at the keyboard, or if we happen to wander away a few feet from the computer when we are logged on to the system.

Monitoring the patron. A number of systems allow you to keep tabs on the quality of the patron's connection during a session—a very useful feature given the unpredictability of Internet connections. But probably the best feature of this type is found in the free instant messaging software . . . which will let you see if the patron is typing a message while you are waiting.

Layout, design, and usability of the librarian's interface. Pay close attention to the layout and design of the librarian interface. How easy is it for the librarian to use the various features and tools of the software? Does the design allow for effective web browsing? In some cases the librarian's browser is so full of tools and icons that you are left with only a tiny window for actual browsing. Those of you working in languages other than English may also want to know whether the librarian's interface can be translated into your language.

Because the librarian's interface generally has to do much more than the patron's browser, there are usually more stringent hardware, operating, and browser requirements on the librarian's side than there are for the patron's. Review the system requirements closely; generally, what you should be looking for is a system that gives you as much flexibility as possible for the kinds of computers that can be used on the librarian side. Also, some systems require that librarians download a large software "client" to their computers. While a software download is not as bad on the librarian's side as it is for the patron, it can still restrict where you can use the software. In general, the less software that has to be downloaded the better.

Librarian Interface Checklist	Y/N	Rank	Comments
Download required?			
Features			
Ability to work with multiple patrons			
Scripts			
Personal, shared, easy to configure			
Bookmarks			
Personal, shared, easy to configure			
Audiovisual alerts			
Patron monitoring features			
Evaluate layout and design of librarian interface			
Interface can be translated into your language			
Librarian hardware requirements			
Librarian operating systems requirements			
Librarian browser requirements			
Librarian connection requirements			
Librarian firewall or network requirements			
System works with adaptive software and devices?			

12. LIBRARIAN TRAINING, SUPPORT, AND DOCUMENTATION

It is becoming increasingly apparent that good virtual reference librarians are made, not born. And the level and quality of the training and support available to those of us who must actually sit down at the terminals and handle the questions can have a major impact on staff morale, the quality of the service we provide, and the overall success of the project. (Training and support issues are covered in greater detail in chapter 3.) In evaluating virtual reference software, the question is, what are the type, level, and quality of the training provided by the vendor, and how much of it will you be left to do on your own? Software vendors vary wildly in this area: with some—like the free instant messaging services, for example—you are entirely on your own. Some vendors offer training on their software, but know nothing about the skills and techniques of virtual reference service. Others provide days of on-site training by experienced virtual reference librarians who cover both the software and online reference techniques, and follow it up with mentored practice sessions and librarian support.

The following are some of the questions you'll want to ask in evaluating the training offered by vendors. What type of training is available and how much is offered? What subjects are covered: software only, or software and the techniques of virtual reference? How is the training offered: by self-study using manuals, CD-ROM or web-based tutorials, live online training, or will they actually send trainers out to your library? How many hours or days of training are offered, and—particularly for larger libraries and consortia—how many staff can be trained? Who does the training, and how much do they know about libraries and virtual reference? Obviously, the more trainers know about virtual reference, the better they can integrate software training with reference practice. How much continuing librarian support does the vendor offer after the initial training sessions? Many vendors offer nothing in this area; some offer "mentored" online practice sessions as librarians are learning the system, and a few have mentor librarians available at all times. Finally, what kind of training manuals and system documentation are available, and how do you get access to them? Here again, some vendors provide extensive training and system manuals with online exercises that librarians can use on their own, while others don't offer any more than a few software help screens.

Librarian Training, Support, and Documentation	Y/N	Rank	Comments
What type of training is offered?			
Software only			
Software and virtual reference			
Number of days or hours offered			
How is training offered? (Some vendors offer more than one option here)			
Self-study			
Live online			
On-site			
What sort of after-training support is available to librarians—guided practice sessions, online mentor librarians, etc.?			
What sorts of training manuals and documentation are available?			

13. ADMINISTRATION

The administrative interface is where you go to set up, configure, and modify the system's software, and where you can monitor and run reports detailing how the system is being used. The real questions you need to ask here are, first, is there an administrative interface to the software at all? This may seem a bit silly, but remember that on instant messaging software and a number of inexpensive chat products, all you have is the basic program that allows you to communicate with the patron. There is nothing for you to set up and you can't change anything about the way the software works or performs on your site, so there is no need for an administrative interface. If the software does offer an administrative interface, then the question is, what can you do with it? This is really a measure of how configurable and customizable the software is, how much of that configuration and customization does the vendor allow you to do on your own, and how much of it do you have to ask the vendor to do for you . . . and at what additional cost?

Administrative interfaces differ substantially from package to package, and it is impossible to cover all the features that might be included, but some of the more important ones are listed below. The important consideration here is that you evaluate the administrative interface according to how you might be using the system, and make sure that the software provides you with the ability to perform routine functions as easily as possible.

Common administrative features include the following ones.

Adding and modifying users and queues. Can you add, modify, and delete librarians and service lines on the system? These are important features because the people using the system can change all the time, as can the service lines or queues you have on your website. So it is nice to be able to add and delete users or access points to your service without having to ask anyone's permission or having to pay for the privilege.

Adding or modifying scripts, bookmarks, and other shared content. Systems that offer shared scripts, bookmarks, and other content often have some way of setting these up through the administrative interface. These things can change frequently, so you want the ability to access and modify them on your own.

System configuration. There are literally thousands of elements in a sophisticated virtual reference system that you might want to modify or configure—everything from the look and feel of your patron log-in screens, to the text of the automated messages the software generates as the patron logs on, to the boilerplate in the e-mail messages the system sends out with virtual reference transcripts. Examine the settings and configuration functions in the administrative interface carefully to see exactly what you are permitted to modify, and note those that are the most important to your operation.

System monitor. Monitoring features allow you to get a real-time look at the vital statistics of your virtual reference service. Many systems will allow you to see which other librarians are logged on, how long they have been on the system, what queues they are monitoring, and whether they are actually in a session at the moment. All of these are very useful features, when you're responsible for managing the system and you want to know if Steve has made it in and logged on for his 5 p.m. shift.

System reporting. Many virtual reference systems collect and store substantial amounts of data on how the service is operating. However, much of this data is only as good as the reporting systems that allow you to view and analyze it. Many systems offer a set of standard reports, and you'll want to take a look at these to see if they provide you with the sort of information you need, and if not, whether they can easily be configured to do so. You'll also want to know how easy it is to get access to the raw data in the underlying database so you can download your information into spreadsheets and other software packages for further analysis. Finally, some vendors serving the library market provide benchmark data that can be helpful in comparing.your system statistics with others.

Special administrative features for consortia. There are a couple of administrative features that are particularly useful for those of you working in shared or consortium reference systems. The first and most important of these is the ability to have a two-tiered administrative system—a library-level administrator who only has the ability to access the setup, configuration, and reporting functions for their own library or institution; and another system administrator(s) level which has access to all of the libraries and functions of the system. This allows members of the consortium to do a lot of their own configuration and reporting without having to ask permission or risk interfering with others on the system. Other administrative features that can be useful in groups or consortia are shared calendars, so that it is easy to tell which library is supposed to be on when; shared policy and procedure documents that reference staff can easily access while on reference sessions; and a shared set of library profiles that allow reference staff ready access to the basic details—hours, databases, link to catalog, etc.—for each participating library.

Administrative Interface	Y/N	Rank	Comments
Administrative interface available?			
Add or modify users or queues			
Add or modify scripts, bookmarks, content			
Other system configuration options—describe:			
System monitoring available?			
What can be monitored?			
System reporting available?			
Types of standard reports			
Data can be exported for further analysis			
Administrative features for consortia			
Two-tiered administrative privileges			
Shared reference calendar			
Shared policy and procedures documents			
Shared library profiles			
Other			

14. LICENSED OR HOSTED

Virtual reference systems come in two basic flavors: licensed, which means that you purchase the software outright and maintain and operate it yourself on your own hardware and network; and hosted (also known as the "ASP model"), where the software, database, and most other system components reside on the vendor's computers and both you and the patron access the software through an Internet browser or some similar "client" interface. With the hosted model, you normally pay the vendor some sort of regular rental fee for access to the software—which is much less than the cost of purchasing the software outright under the licensed model—but you pay it for as long as you use the software.

Because virtual reference is still a new and unproven field, and because good virtual reference software is expensive to purchase and maintain, so far, most libraries have opted for the hosted approach. Also, most free software options like the instant messaging programs are based on a hosted model. However, the hosted model introduces some special concerns for libraries that you should address before opting for a hosted system. First off, since the software and the database—including your patron data—reside on the vendor's servers, you need to be sure just who owns that data, who has access to it, and what use they are permitted to make of it. These are not insignificant issues. If you are working in a secure government facility or a corporate library with a lot of proprietary data, the fact that you've got a database sitting out on someone else's servers with verbatim transcripts of every reference question you ever answered could seriously compromise your data security. And the rest of us should be concerned that our patrons' privacy is adequately protected and that we have access to and control over the data stored on the vendor's servers. So when you are considering a hosted system, make sure you carefully review the legal details of your agreement to see who has control of the data.

Vendor reliability is another important consideration for hosted systems. Remember that you are relying on the vendor to keep the software up and running on its servers, so you will want to assure yourself that it is capable of doing that. There are a variety of criteria you can use to evaluate this, including the redundancy of the vendor's hardware, software, and network setup (have your IT department speak to their IT department); operational data, like the amount of downtime actually experienced over the past year; and general "financial health" information such as whether the vendor is large or small, has it been around some time, and is it financially stable? Finally, because all communication from both you and the patron will be going through the vendor's servers, it may be important where those servers are located. The Internet is pretty fast, but real-time applications can be very demanding, and sometimes if the geographic distance between the library and those servers is too great, it can slow down system performance. The best way to check this is to actually try the system and see how it responds at different times of day. You may also want to check with the vendor to see where its servers are located.

If you opt to purchase the software under the licensed model, you have another set of concerns. In the first place, you'll want to know what sort of hardware and software are required, for both the virtual reference software itself and any of the auxiliary applications that may be required (most virtual reference systems require auxiliary software packages such as SQL databases in addition to what you buy from the vendor). You will also want to check to make sure that your own system networks, firewalls, and software do not conflict with the software, that you have adequate connections to the Internet, and that you have the staff to keep the system up and running and to provide your own end-user technical support. Be sure not to underestimate the staffing, because virtual reference systems can require a lot of care and feeding, and good technical support is essential.

No matter which approach you take, you will want to check on the level of technical support available from the vendor. What type of support is available, what hours is it available, who can request it (identified technical contacts only, any librarian, just the project manager), and how is it accessed (800 number, e-mail, error report form in software, etc.)? Finally, you may want to ask what sort of compensation is available for the library if the system does go down or becomes unusable.

Licensed or Hosted	**Y/N**	**Rank**	**Comments**
Hosted model			
Data security			
Who owns your data?			
Who has access to it?			
Limitations on use			

Licensed or Hosted	Y/N	Rank	Comments
Hosted model (cont'd)			
System reliability			
Hosted system redundancy			
Reported system downtime			
Vendor financial stability			
Geographic issues			
Where are vendor's servers located?			
Licensed model			
Hardware requirements			
Software requirements			
Network and connection requirements			
Staffing requirements			
Technical support			
What level of support is available?			
Who can use it?			
What hours is it available?			
How do you access it?			

15. QUEUING AND ROUTING STRUCTURE

The queuing and routing structure describes how patrons and librarians are connected with one another on the system. It is a critical factor in selecting software, because it ultimately determines what kind of reference service you can build with it. You would not think of equipping a large library that receives hundreds of calls per day with a single-line home phone system; on the other hand, automatic call distribution, conference and transfer features, music on hold, and multiline phones may be a little overkill for a small system where you are not expecting to get more than a few calls per day. And the telephone analogy is appropriate, because most virtual reference services follow telephone system models.

No matter how sophisticated your system, patrons first initiate a call by clicking on a link on your library website. It's how the software handles the call after that where the differences begin to appear.

Many of the instant messaging programs that are designed for friendly chats, or much of the remote control software that is intended for occasional use in technical support, operate just like single-line home telephone systems. Only one librarian can be on it at a time, and if a patron calls in while that librarian is already on a call, they will get a busy signal. These systems will work effectively with low-volume reference services where you're getting only a few questions per day and you don't need to have more than one librarian at a time logged in.

Web conferencing software and many courseware products work in much the same way, except that, in this case, the patron is connected to the equivalent of a telephone conference call where there may be many others on the same session at the same time. This is a nice feature for online programming and classroom instruction, but it is not particularly useful for one-on-one reference sessions.

Finally, there are the virtual reference systems modeled after telephone call centers. These systems are designed for reference services where there may be multiple patrons calling in at the same time, and multiple librarians logged on to help them. With these systems, when a call comes in from your website, it is first sent to an "automatic call distributor" that monitors who's logged on and not in a call, and routes the question to the next available librarian. If all librarians are busy, the patron is placed on hold and automatically routed to the first librarian that is free.

This is a basic description of how the call center model works, but there can be significant differences in the way various software applications implement it. The following are some of the more important features you'll want to look for.

Routing methods. Most systems only route calls to the next available librarian, but some have more sophisticated algorithms that help balance the question load across all staff logged on. For example, if two librarians are available, some systems can route the call to the one that has handled the fewest calls during the shift. Other systems can use skills-based routing to route a question to the most appropriate librarian based on the subject matter, language, academic level, or other criteria.

Queues. Queues are the "telephone lines" patrons use to access your system, and how you can set them up and what features are associated with them can be very important in system design. Some systems permit you to customize the software at the queue level, so that a queue can have its own look and feel, as well as a set of shared scripts, bookmarks, and other content. This can be a particularly useful feature in consortia where each library on the system could have its own queue, and hence its own look and feel, and yet still share reference services with others using the software.

Messages. What kind of messages does the system give to patrons logging on? What sort of message do they get if the service is closed or if they are put on hold, and can the system provide an estimate for the amount of time they will be on hold? Can these messages be customized for your library?

Conference and transfer. Does the software allow reference staff to transfer calls to someone else on the system, or to conference another librarian into a call? If so, does the system have a "warm transfer" capability where the librarian receiving the call has access to a full transcript of the call up to that point?

Outbound calls. So far, we have focused on systems that are designed to handle inbound calls—that is, the patron has to take the initiative to contact you. However, there are a number of packages on the market that will track people visiting your library's website, and allow you to initiate (or try to initiate) an outbound call to them while they are on the site. Some programs handle this pretty unobtrusively, by floating a little icon across the patron's screen that might say something like "If you need help, click here." Others can be quite blatant about it, like "Hi, I'm a librarian, and it looks like you could use some help." So far, libraries have tended to shy away from outbound calls because they are wisely worried about patron reaction. However, others have pointed out that it is really not all that much different from offering to help a patron you run across in the stacks. If it can be proven that patrons do not object to being contacted while they are on your website, outbound calls may turn out to be a valuable way of marketing virtual reference services.

Queuing and Routing Structure	**Y/N**	**Rank**	**Comments**
Multiple librarians can be logged on?			
Routing method			
Next available librarian			
Load-balancing			
Skills-based			
Messages			
Automatic messages on hold			
Automatic closed messages			
Others			
Messages customizable by queue			
Queues			
System supports multiple queues			
What features can be customized at queue level?			
Librarians can monitor more than one queue			

Queuing and Routing Structure	Y/N	Rank	Comments
Conference and transfer			
Calls can be transferred to another librarian			
Other librarians can be conferenced in to a call			
Warm transfers available			
Outbound calls			

16. CUSTOMIZATION

An important consideration in selecting virtual reference software is how much you can customize the software to suit the needs of your library. The virtual reference software packages currently on the market differ substantially in this area. Some programs—particularly the commercial instant messaging programs—must be used pretty much as is, and offer no customization whatsoever. Others may allow you to customize some aspects of the system, but require you to use their logos and patron interface in order to create some brand awareness. But there are also plenty of systems that allow you to customize every feature of the software, and a few that even allow you to alter the source code.

There is no room here to come up with a complete list of every feature that could be customized, and in theory, anyway, almost every feature and function we've discussed so far could be altered to fit your needs. The important point is that you should keep the potential for customization in mind as you are reviewing all the features of virtual reference systems—and particularly those which involve the patron interface and other areas that affect the public. Buying a good virtual reference system is a lot like buying an expensive suit: you will be investing a lot of time, money, and your library's goodwill in it, and you have a right to ask that it be tailored to fit your needs as much as possible.

Customization	Y/N	Rank	Comments
What elements of the software can be customized for your application?			

APPENDIX B

SAMPLE PRE-EMPLOYMENT SCREENING TEST AND KEY

This test is given to applicants to LSSI's Web Reference Center to help determine their aptitude for virtual reference. The timed reference assignment is conducted via e-mail and must be completed within a two-hour period. The assignment includes two parts: part 1 focuses on the reference interview; and part 2 focuses on responding to reference questions. For a full description and explanation of this test as administered by LSSI, see the subsection "Pre-employment Screening Test" in chapter 3.

[YOUR NAME]
REFERENCE QUESTIONS

Please return within 2 hours of receipt.
You may return the assignment as an e-mail attachment (preferred) or in the text of an e-mail.

Part 1

Create reference interview questions for the following situations, if necessary. You do not need to answer the question.

1. I need the definition of the word "Milanooka." I think it's an American Indian word. It was my grandmother's last name.
   Question from a public library general reference queue.

2. Why are there so many foreigners in the medical profession and not enough American doctors within the United States?
   Question from a public library general reference queue.
3. I am writing a paper on educating foreign children and where the funding should come from. I need a few resources! Thank you!
   Question from a student at a university.

Part 2

At the Web Reference Center we use free resources and resources from our client libraries to respond to patrons' queries. Put yourself in the shoes of a Web Reference Center librarian and respond to the questions below.

You will not have access to the proprietary databases of the libraries mentioned below, but you can visit the websites for those libraries to see what they have. In many cases, free web resources will be very helpful in responding to the question.

Include any reference interview questions you would ask (if necessary) given the opportunity.

Describe your search strategy and the rationale for your approach. Please include URLs consulted, even if they result in no hits.

Include a statement to the patron recommending further search strategies if necessary.

Purpose: I'd like to see how you think as you approach these questions. None of the questions are tricks, and there is no single "right" answer.

1. I'm looking for the movie version of *For Whom the Bell Tolls* with Gary Cooper. I'd like to watch it this weekend.
   Question from general reference queue, Cleveland Public Library, http://www.cpl.org.
2. I've heard about these new digital hearing aids. I have an old-style one. These digital hearing aids cost a lot, thousands of dollars rather than hundreds of dollars (like the one I have), and so I'm wondering if the digital aid is worth the price?
   Question from general reference queue, Cleveland Public Library, http://www.cpl.org.

3. I am doing a persuasive research paper on whether "the medical benefits of embryonic stem cell research are worthwhile and deserve federal funding." I have tried different electronic resources and I am having trouble finding journals, articles, books, etc. Could you please lead me in the right direction? Thanking you in advance for your time.

   Question from a patron using the South Jersey Regional Library Cooperative online reference service. Her public library is http://www.camden.lib.nj.us/.

4. Where can I access a virtual landscape architecture program to use online for free?

   Question from a Denver Public Library patron, http://www.denver.lib.co.us/.

5. I am looking for information about *Funnyhouse of a Negro* by Adrienne Kennedy. I am supposed to find criticisms of the work, but I can't find anything. Do you have any suggestions?

   Question from a student at Bradley University, http://www.bradley.edu/irt/lib/.

REFERENCE QUESTIONS: RESPONSE KEY

Part 1

Reference Interview. Key questions are listed below. We are looking for these or variations which draw out the same information.

1. I need the definition of the word "Milanooka." I think it's an American Indian word. It was my grandmother's last name.

   What makes you think it is an American Indian word?

   Do you know if your grandmother belonged to a tribe? If so, what was its name?

   Where did your grandmother live? State or geographic area.

   What do you know about your Native American ancestry?

   Are you certain the spelling is "Milanooka"? The patron may be spelling it phonetically.

2. Why are there so many foreigners in the medical profession and not enough American doctors within the United States?

    Where did you obtain the information that there are "so many foreigners" and "not enough American doctors within the United States"?

    How are you defining "foreigner"?

    How are you defining "American"?

    You refer to the "medical profession" and you mention doctors. Are you thinking only of doctors, or of other members of the medical profession such as nurses, physicians' assistants, etc.?

3. I am writing a paper on educating foreign children and where the funding should come from. I need a few resources.

    How are you defining foreign children?

    Are you interested in educating children in the United States or in other countries?

    Are you interested in sources of funding available in the United States or in other countries?

    What class is this for? What level is the class?

Part 2

Include any reference interview questions you would ask (if necessary) given the opportunity.

Describe your search strategy and the rationale for your approach. Please include URLs consulted, even if they result in no hits.

Include a statement to the patron recommending further search strategies if necessary.

1. I'm looking for the movie version of *For Whom the Bell Tolls* with Gary Cooper. I'd like to watch it this weekend.

    Question from general reference queue, Cleveland Public Library, http://www.cpl.org.

    Reference interview questions not really necessary.

    A number of Cleveland Public Library (CPL) branches have the video; it is the version with Gary Cooper.

Further research strategy

Could include finding out what branch library the patron uses and directing the patron to the appropriate branch; recommending interlibrary loan of video if appropriate.

2. I've heard about these new digital hearing aids. I have an old-style one. These digital hearing aids cost a lot, thousands of dollars rather than hundreds of dollars (like the one I have), and so I'm wondering if the digital aid is worth the price?

   Question from general reference queue, Cleveland Public Library, http://www.cpl.org.

Reference interview questions

Probably not necessary, but you might try to ascertain whether or not the patron has done any reading on the topic yet; by making this inquiry and establishing a dialogue, you might also discover, by the patron's response, his or her reading or comprehension level. Regardless, a reasonable response to this question is to locate materials directed at consumers, not professionals.

Answer

Should avoid commercial sites. Most have a bias toward their own product(s).

Should search for consumer information v. professional-level papers.

Examples of relevant information freely accessible on the Web

American Speech Language Hearing Association (ASHA) will come up from a Google search, and it has a number of articles reviewing the features and functionality of digital v. analog hearing aids.

"Hearing Aids, Myths and Facts" from ASHA looks very good: http://www.asha.org/hearing/rehab/aid_myth_fact.cfm.

American Academy of Audiology: This site includes a consumer information section, including info on how to purchase a hearing aid, and FAQs about hearing aids, including an explanation of the various types—analog, digital, etc.: http://www.audiology.org/consumer/guides/hafaq.php.

Further research strategy

Recommend consumer databases or general health databases at CPL such as Masterfile (via Ebsco); Health and Wellness Resource Center; MDX Health Digest; Netwellness (all found by searching the CPL databases by the subject "health").

3. I am doing a persuasive research paper on whether "the medical benefits of embryonic stem cell research are worthwhile and deserve federal funding." I have tried different electronic resources and I am having trouble finding journals, articles, books, etc. Could you please lead me in the right direction? Thanking you in advance for your time.

   Question from a patron using the South Jersey Regional Library Cooperative (SJRLC) online reference service. Her public library is http://www.camden.lib.nj.us/.

   Reference interview questions

   Might be good to find out if the patron is interested in advocating for or against stem cell research. Regardless, the following search strategies provide good info.

   Examples of relevant information freely accessible on the Web

   There is a Union catalog for SJRLC libraries. A keyword search on "embryonic stem cell" will bring up one title, but two subject headings are associated with the concept of stem cell research:

   Human embryo—research—moral and ethical aspects.

   Stem cells—research—moral and ethical aspects.

   By searching both of these subject headings, you'll find three titles in the SJRLC system.

   Google search: "stem cell (pros and cons)" provides link to JAMA article: http://jama.ama-assn.org/issues/v284n6/fpdf/jmn0809.pdf.

   Google search also finds: http://directory.google.com/Top/Society/Issues/Science_and_Technology/Biotechnology/Stem_Cell_Research/, which includes links to news coverage of the topic from CNN, BBC, and CBC; statements from organizations like NIH, but also Christian organizations, etc. Certainly fodder for thought about whether the research should be government funded.

NIH has a wealth of information on this topic: http://www.nih.gov/news/stemcell/.

Joint Steering Committee for Public Policy, coalition of four biomedical research societies. Some good info here.

Further research strategy

Recommend databases at the library and suggest search terms. You might want to alert the patron to the fact that she should try variations on her terms, e.g., "embryo," "embryos," "embryonic"; "stem cell" and "stem cells." All of these things make a difference to the results gathered from a web search engine or database. Also, at the core of this debate is an ethical question, so advise the patron to include "ethical," "ethics," or "ethic" in her search.

4. Where can I access a virtual landscape architecture program to use online for free?

Question from a Denver Public Library patron, http://www.denver.lib.co.us/.

Reference interview questions

On its face, the question is straightforward, but you might want to find out if the patron is looking for this info as a student—if so, is he studying architecture or urban planning or garden/landscape design—or as an individual interested in simply planning a garden. If you have no idea about "landscape architecture," educate yourself by doing a quick Google search.

Answer/Examples of relevant info freely accessible on the Web

Key here is the patron's interest in locating a "free" program.

A search of "landscape architecture freeware" in Google will bring up relevant sites, including http://www.asla.org/lamag/archive.html, which has a link to "Shareware, freeware, trialware, and demoware": http://www.asla.org/nonmembers/ SHRWRlst.htm.

There are other search strategies, of course. The point here was to find at least one freeware site for the patron.

Further research strategy

None suggested, but if you did not find a freeware site, then I would have liked you to have suggested a way for the patron to have pursued research on his own. You might recommend the patron look at commercial sites for various landscape architecture software programs, and suggest he inquire about trial periods. Alternatively, refer the patron to a Denver area school where landscape architecture is taught.

5. I am looking for information about *Funnyhouse of a Negro* by Adrienne Kennedy. I am supposed to find criticisms of the work, but I can't find anything. Do you have any suggestions?

   Question from a student at Bradley University, http://www.bradley.edu/irt/lib/.

Reference questions

You might want to confirm whether this is a novel, short story, play, or poem. Since you cannot ask the student, you can ascertain this on your own. The form of the piece may dictate how and where you look for info about it.

What class is the student studying the piece for? The student's academic level and ability to express herself may dictate the resources you advise her to use. The *MLA Style Manual*, for example, is generally too complex for first- or second-year students.

Answer/Examples of relevant info freely accessible on the Web

Websites with criticism or bibliographies of Kennedy's work. There are quite a few good ones.

Rutgers site: http://www.scils.rutgers.edu/~cybers/fun.html includes production history of *Funnyhouse* as well as a brief excerpt from *Contemporary Authors* entry on Kennedy.

Rutgers site: http://www.scils.rutgers.edu/~cybers/kennedy2.html includes bibliography of articles specifically about Kennedy.

You could use this list to refer the patron to articles at Bradley library in print subscriptions.

http://www.umich.edu/~eng499/people/kennedy.html includes a brief bio of Kennedy and links to a bibliography on black drama, theatre, and Afro-American literature (general).

You should also recommend specific databases at Bradley where the patron could search for online, full-text articles.

You could suggest reference books at Bradley on African-American drama, African-American women writers, African-American literature. It is sometimes difficult to find these reference materials in catalogs because of the subject headings: "Black" has been replaced largely by "African-American."

http://www.upress.umn.edu/Books/B/bryant_jackson_intersectin.html provides an overview of a 1992 book of criticism on Kennedy's work. Does Bradley have it? If not, suggest interlibrary loan.

Free, online: 26-page critical article on *Funnyhouse* from the journal *Post Identity*, a refereed journal of the humanities, at http://liberalarts.udmercy.edu/pi/PI1.1/PI11_Thompson.pdf.

Another full-text article: http://www.amrep.org/past/ohio/ohio1.html, by Werner Sollors, who is professor of English literature and professor of Afro-American studies at Harvard University. The article is authoritative: "These remarks are adapted from the introduction to the forthcoming *Adrienne Kennedy Reader* (Minnesota: University of Minnesota Press, 2001). Minnesota Press has in the past decade published much of Kennedy's works, including *The Alexander Plays*."

Catalog search

Adrienne Kennedy does not appear in the Bradley catalog as an individual subject heading; so they don't have books focusing exclusively on her. However . . .

There are ten titles with a relevant subject: American drama—African-American authors—History and criticism. The books might contain essays on Kennedy's work; the only way to verify is to look at index of book—a point well worth making to the patron.

A title of particular interest, given the time period Kennedy's plays were written and performed: *Black Theatre in the 1960s and 1970s: An Historical, Critical Analysis of the Movement,* by Mance Williams.

Reference books about black women authors, playwrights, drama, literature.

VIRTUAL REFERENCE SERVICES BIBLIOGRAPHY

An Abridged Version of the Bibliography

by Bernie Sloan

Abram, Stephen. "Planning for the Next Wave of Convergence." *Computers in Libraries* 20, no. 4 (April 2000): 46–53.

Albano, Jessica, Adam Hall, and Lorena O'English. "The Electronic Information Desk: Communication Made Virtual." Paper presented at Facets of Digital Reference Service: The Virtual Reference Desk Second Annual Digital Reference Conference, Seattle, Wash., 16–17 October 2000. Available at http://www.vrd.org/conferences/VRD2000/proceedings/albano-hall-oenglish.shtml.

Ammentorp, Steen, and Marianne Hummelshoj. "Ask a Librarian: Web-Based Reference Question Services: A Model for Development." Paper presented at the 11th Nordic Conference on Information and Documentation, Reykjavik, Iceland, 30 May–1 June 2001. Available at http://www.bokis.is/iod2001/papers/Ammentorp_paper.doc.

Anderson, Eric, Josh Boyer, and Karen Ciccone. "Remote Reference Services at the North Carolina State University Libraries." Paper presented at Facets of Digital Reference Service: The Virtual Reference Desk Second Annual Digital Reference Conference, Seattle, Wash., 16–17 October 2000. Available at http://www.vrd.org/conferences/VRD2000/proceedings/boyer-anderson-ciccone12–14.shtml.

This bibliography is an abbreviated version of the bibliography maintained by Bernie Sloan at http://www.lis.uiuc.edu/~b-sloan/digiref.html. Special thanks go to Kristina Womack of the LSSI Web Reference Center for her help in editing the bibliography and making it ready for publication.

Bell, M. M. "Managing Reference E-Mail in an Archival Setting: Tools for the Increasing Number of Reference Queries." *College and Research Libraries News* 63, no. 2 (2002): 99–101.

Bennett, Blythe A. "Developing an Internet-Based Reference Service." In *The Cybrarian's Manual 2,* edited by Pat Ensor, 159–69. Chicago: American Library Association, 2000.

Bivens-Tatum, Wayne. "Expert Services on the Web: The Commercial Competition for Libraries." *College and Research Libraries News* 62, no. 7 (July/August 2001): 714–16.

Borchardt, Karen, and Jennifer Croud. "Digital Reference Service: A New Service or the Next Logical Step?" Paper presented at Educause in Australasia 2001, Gold Coast, Queensland, Australia, 20–23 May 2001. Available at http://www.library.uq.edu.au/papers/digitalref.doc.

Bossueau, D. L. "Digital Reference Services: Virtual or Real?" *Information Management Report* (October 2001): 1–4.

Boyer, Joshua. "Virtual Reference at the NCSU Libraries: The First One Hundred Days." *Information Technology and Libraries* 20, no. 3 (September 2001): 122–28. Available at http://www.lita.org/ital/2003_boyer.html/.

Bradbury, David, and Georgina Payne. "The OPAL Project: Developing an Online Digital Reference Service for Distance Learners." *Library Hi Tech News* 18, no. 9 (2001): 28–29.

Brandt, D. Scott. "E-Mail Makes the World Go 'Round." *Computers in Libraries* 20, no. 10 (November/December 2000). Available at http://www.infotoday.com/cilmag/nov00/brandt.htm.

Breeding, Marshall. "Providing Virtual Reference Service." *Information Today* 18, no. 4 (1 April 2000): 42–43.

Bristow, Ann, and Jian Liu. "Academic Reference Service in the Web Environment." Paper partially presented at IOLUG Fall Program, Indianapolis, Ind., 22 October 1999, and at CIC Online Reference Services Workshop, Madison, Wis., 3–4 May 2001. Available at http://www.indiana.edu/~librcsd/reference/email/03.html.

Broughton, Kelly. "Our Experiment in Online, Real-Time Reference." *Computers in Libraries* 21, no. 4 (April 2001): 26–31. Available at http://www.infotoday.com/cilmag/apr01/broughton.htm.

Broughton, Kelly, Stefanie Dennis Hunker, and Carol A. Singer. "Why Use Web Contact Center Software for Digital Reference?" *Internet Reference Services Quarterly* 6, no. 2 (2001): 1–12.

Bush, Vannevar. "As We May Think." *Atlantic Monthly,* July 1945. Available at http://www.theatlantic.com/unbound/flashbks/computer/bushf.htm.

Bushallow-Wilber, Laura, Gemma DeVinney, and Fritz Whitcomb. "Electronic Mail Reference Service: A Study." *RQ* 35, no. 3 (spring 1996): 359–63.

Carlson, Scott. "New Service Allows the Public to Pose Reference Questions without Visiting the Library." *Chronicle of Higher Education* (31 May 2002). Available at http://chronicle.com/free/2002/05/2002053101t.htm.

Carter, David S., and Joseph Janes. "Unobtrusive Data Analysis of Digital Reference Questions and Service at the Internet Public Library: An Exploratory Study." *Library Trends* 49, no. 2 (fall 2000): 251–65.

Chowdhury, G. G. "Digital Libraries and Reference Services: Present and Future." *Journal of Documentation* 58, no. 3 (2002): 258–83.

Ciccone, Karen. "Virtual Reference, Today and Tomorrow." *Information Technology and Libraries* 20, no. 3 (September 2001): 120–21. Available at http://www.lita.org/ital/2003_editorial.html.

Cichanowicz, Edana McCaffery. "Sunday Night Live! An Experiment in Live Reference Chat." *NyLink Connection* 3, no. 1 (spring 2001): 8–9. Available at http://nylink.suny.edu/docu/nc/NCspr01.pdf. (Link is to entire issue.)

———. "Sunday Night Live!—An Experiment in Real Time Reference Chat—On a Shoestring Budget." *Charleston Advisor* 2, no. 4 (15 April 2001): 49–51. Available at http://www.charlestonco.com/features.cfm?id=59&type=fr.

Coffman, Steve. "Distance Education and Virtual Reference: Where Are We Headed?" *Computers in Libraries* 31, no. 5 (April 2001): 66–69. Available at http://www.infotoday.com/cilmag/apr01/coffman.htm.

———. "So You Want to Do Virtual Reference?" *Public Libraries* Supplement (E-Libraries issue) (September/October 2001): 14–20.

———. "We'll Take It from Here: Further Developments We'd Like to See in Virtual Reference Software." *Information Technology and Libraries* 20, no. 3 (September 2001): 149–53. Available at http://www.lita.org/ital/2003_coffman.html/.

———. "What's Wrong with Collaborative Digital Reference?" *American Libraries* 33, no. 11 (December 2002): 56–59.

Coffman, Steve, and Susan McGlamery. "The Librarian and Mr. Jeeves." *American Libraries* 31, no. 5 (May 2000): 66–69.

Coffman, Steve, and Matthew L. Saxton. "Staffing the Reference Desk in the Largely-Digital Library." *Reference Librarian* 66 (1999): 141–63.

Colvin, Gloria. "Remote, Accessible, and on Call: Reference Librarians Go Live." *Florida Libraries* 44, no. 1 (spring 2001): 10–12. Available at http://www.flalib.org/library/fla/florlibs/44_1.pdf.

Constantine, Paul. "Digital Reference in an Academic Library." Paper presented at Building the Virtual Reference Desk in a 24/7 World, Library of Congress, Washington, D.C., 12 January 2001. Available at http://www.loc.gov/rr/digiref/webcasts/constantine/constantine.html.

Cunningham, Sally Jo. "Providing Internet Reference Service for the New Zealand Digital Library: Gaining Insight into the User Base for a Digital Library." Department of Computer Science, University of Waikato, New Zealand. Available at http://web.simmons.edu/~chen/nit/NIT'98/98-027-Cunningham.html.

Curtis, Susan, et al. "Cooperative Reference: Is There a Consortium Model?" *Reference and User Services Quarterly* 41, no. 4 (summer 2002): 344–49.

D'Angelo, Barbara, and Barry Maid. "Virtual Classroom, Virtual Library: Library Services for an Online Writing Laboratory." *Reference and User Services Quarterly* 39, no. 3 (spring 2000): 278–83.

Daugaard, Vera. "Net Librarian: A Danish National Online Information Service." Paper presented at Facets of Digital Reference Service: The Virtual Reference Desk Second Annual Digital Reference Conference, Seattle, Wash., 16–17 October 2000. Available at http://www.vrd.org/conferences/VRD2000/proceedings/Daugaard12-14.shtml.

Davenport, Elisabeth, and Rob Procter. "The Situated Intermediary: Remote Advice Giving in a Distributed Reference Environment." In *Proceedings of the Eighteenth National Online Meeting*. Medford, N.J.: Information Today, 1997.

DeCandido, GraceAnne A. "E-Reference: Closing in on 24/7." *Public Library Association Tech Notes* (March 2001). Available at http://www.pla.org/technotes/ereference.html.

Dee, Cheryl. "Current Environment of Hospital Library Reference: Part 2—Trends for the Future." *Medical Reference Services Quarterly* 20, no. 1 (spring 2001): 69–78.

Deegan, Eileen. "Conducting the Reference Interview by E-Mail and the Intranet." Paper presented at the SLA Annual Conference, Philadelphia, Pa., 12 June 2000. Available at http://www.library.northwestern.edu/transportation/slatran/philpresents/DeeganPresentation.htm.

Dent, V. F. "Technology Provides Innovative Reference Services at University of Michigan Libraries." *Research Strategies* 17, no. 2 (second quarter 2000): 187–93.

Diamond, Wendy, and Barbara Pease. "Digital Reference: A Case Study of Question Types in an Academic Library." *Reference Services Review* 29, no. 3 (2001): 210–18.

Dilevko, Juris. "An Ideological Analysis of Digital Reference Service Models." *Library Trends* 50, no. 2 (fall 2001): 218–44.

Dougherty, Richard M. "Reference around the Clock: Is It in Your Future?" *American Libraries* 33, no. 5 (May 2002): 44–46.

Duggan, James E. "The New Reference Librarian: Using Technology to Deliver Reference." *Legal Reference Services Quarterly* 19, no. 3/4 (2001): 195–202.

Dysart, Jane I., and Rebecca J. Jones. "Tools for the Future: Recreating or 'Renovating' Information Services Using New Technologies." *Computers in Libraries* 15, no. 1 (January 1995): 16–19.

Eichler, Linda, and Michael Halperin. "LivePerson: Keeping Reference Alive and Clicking." *Econtent* 23, no. 3 (June 2000): 63–66. Available at http://www.ecmag.net/awards/award13.html.

Ellis, Lisa, and Stephen Francoeur. "Applying Information Competency to Digital Reference." Paper presented at the 67th IFLA Council and

General Conference, Boston, Mass., 16–25 August 2001. Available at http://www.ifla.org/IV/ifla67/papers/057-98e.pdf.

Ercegovac, Zorana. "Collaborative E-Reference: A Research Agenda." Paper presented at the 67th IFLA Council and General Conference, Boston, Mass., 16–25 August 2001. Available at http://www.ifla.org/IV/ifla67/papers/058-98e.pdf.

"Expanding Reference Services for the University of California: A White Paper on the Relevance of Digital Reference Service to the UC Libraries." 9 November 2001. Available at http://www.slp.ucop.edu/sopag/DigitalReference.pdf.

Fagan, Judy Condit, and Michele Calloway. "Creating an Instant Messaging Reference System." *Information Technology and Libraries* 20, no. 4 (December 2001): 202–12. Available at http://www.lita.org/ital/2004_fagan.html.

Feldman, Susan. "The Answer Machine." *Searcher* 8, no. 1 (January 2000). Available at http://www.infotoday.com/searcher/jan00/feldman.htm.

Fiander, M. "Virtual Reference: A Letter from North America." *Cultivate Interactive* 6, no. 11 (February 2002). Available at http://www.cultivate-int.org/issue6/reference/.

Fishman, Diane L. "Managing the Virtual Reference Desk: How to Plan an Effective E-Mail Reference System." *Medical Reference Services Quarterly* 17, no. 1 (spring 1998): 1–10.

Fogg, Anita. "The University of Ballarat's Development of an Electronic Reference Form." Paper presented at CAVAL (Cooperative Action by Victorian Academic Libraries), Reference Interest Group, Forum—"The Virtual Reference Desk," State Library of Victoria, Melbourne, Australia, 9 July 1999. Available at http://home.vicnet.net.au/~caval/fogg.htm.

Foley, Marianne. "Instant Messaging Reference in an Academic Library: A Case Study." *College and Research Libraries* 63, no. 1 (January 2002): 36–45.

Folger, Kathleen M. "The Virtual Librarian: Using Desktop Videoconferencing to Provide Interactive Reference Service Assistance." Paper presented at the 1997 ACRL Annual Conference, Nashville, Tenn., 11–14 April 1997. Available at http://www.ala.org/acrl/paperhtm/a09.html.

Foster, Janet B. "Web Reference: A Virtual Reality." *Public Libraries* 38, no. 2 (1999): 94–95.

Francoeur, Stephen. "An Analytical Survey of Chat Reference Services." *Reference Services Review* 29, no. 3 (2001): 189–203.

Frank, Ilene B. "E-Mail Reference Service at the University of South Florida: A Well-Kept Secret." *Art Documentation* 17, no. 1 (1998): 8–9.

Fritch, John W., and Scott B. Mandernack. "The Emerging Reference Paradigm: A Vision of Reference Services in a Complex Information Environment." *Library Trends* 50, no. 2 (fall 2001): 286–305.

Fullerton, Vera. "E-Mail Reference: Refocus and Revise. Experiences from Gelman Library." Paper presented at the 67th IFLA Council and General Conference, Boston, Mass., 16–25 August 2001. Available at http://www.ifla.org/IV/ifla67/papers/056-98e.pdf.

Gardner, Melanie A., JoAnn Devries, and Cidy Kaag. "How Many Trees in a Forest: Creating Digital Reference Services in Agriculture." Paper presented at Facets of Digital Reference Service: The Virtual Reference Desk Second Annual Digital Reference Conference, Seattle, Wash., 16–17 October 2000. Available at http://www.vrd.org/conferences/VRD2000/proceedings/gardner-devries-kaag2-01.shtml.

Garnsey, Beth A., and Ronald R. Powell. "Electronic Mail Reference Services in the Public Library." *Reference and User Services Quarterly* 39, no. 3 (spring 2000): 245–54.

Giannini, Tula. "Rethinking the Reference Interview—From Interpersonal Communication to Online Information Process." *Proceedings of the ASIS Annual Meeting* 36 (1999): 373–80.

Gray, Suzanne M. "Virtual Reference Services Directions and Agendas." *Reference and User Services Quarterly* 39, no. 4 (summer 2000): 365–75.

Gross, Melissa, Charles McClure, and R. David Lankes. "Assessing Quality in Digital Reference Services: Overview of Key Literature on Digital Reference." Information Use Management and Policy Institute, Florida State University, November 2001. Available at http://dlis.dos.state.fl.us/bld/Research_Office/VRDphaseII.LitReview.doc.

Grudin, Jonathan. "Groupware and Social Dynamics: Eight Challenges for Developers." *CACM94 Proceedings*. Available at http://www.ics.uci.edu/~grudin/Papers/CACM94/cacm94.html.

Grudin, Jonathan, and Leysia Palen. "Why Groupware Succeeds: Discretion or Mandate?" *ECSCW95 Proceedings*. Available at http://www.ics.uci.edu/~grudin/Papers/ECSCW95/ECSCW.html.

Guenther, Kim. "Know Thy Remote Users." *Computers in Libraries* 21, no. 4 (April 2001): 52–55.

Haines, Annette. "Web Forms: Improving, Expanding, and Promoting Remote Reference Services." *College and Research Libraries* 60, no. 4 (1999): 271–72.

Heilig, Jean M. "E-Global Library: The Academic Campus Library Meets the Internet." *Searcher* 9, no. 6 (June 2001): 34–42.

———. "Virtual Reference at Jones University." *Colorado Libraries* 27, no. 2 (summer 2001): 35–37.

Helfer, Doris Small. "Virtual Reference in Libraries: Remote Patrons Heading Your Way?" *Searcher* 9, no. 2 (February 2001): 67–70.

Henry, Marcia. "The Future of the Academic Reference Desk in Virtual Library Services: Responses from University, Public, and Community College Libraries." Paper presented at Internet Librarian 2001, Pasadena, Calif., 6 November 2001. Available at http://library.csun.edu/mhenry/il2001.html.

Henson, Bruce, and Kathy Gillespie Tomajko. "Electronic Reference Services: Opportunities and Challenges." *Journal of Educational Media and Library Sciences* 38, no. 2 (December 2000): 113–21.

Hert, Carol A. "Information Seeking and User-Intermediary Interactions: Informing the Design of Digital Reference Services." Paper presented at Facets of Digital Reference Service: The Virtual Reference Desk Second Annual Digital Reference Conference, Seattle, Wash., 16–17 October 2000. Available at http://www.vrd.org/conferences/VRD2000/proceedings/Hert12-14.shtml.

Hinton, Danielle, and Lou McGill. "Chat to a Librarian: Twenty-First Century Reference for Distance Learners." *Vine* 122 (March 2001): 59–64.

Hoag, Tara J., and Edana McCaffery Cichanowicz. "Going Prime Time with Live Chat Reference." *Computers in Libraries* 21, no. 8 (September 2001): 40–45.

Hodges, Pauline R. "Reference in the Age of Automation: Changes in Reference Service at Chemical Abstracts Service Library." *Special Libraries* 80, no. 4 (1989): 251–57.

Hodges, Ruth A. "Assessing Digital Reference." *LIBRI* 52, no. 3 (September 2002): 157–68.

Hohmann, Laura. "Providing Reference Services over the Internet." *Colorado Libraries* (Summer 2000): 16–18.

Holmer, Susan E., and Janie B. Silveria. "Food for Thought at the QandAcafé." Paper presented at Information Strategies 2001, Fort Myers, Fla., 14–16 November 2001. Available at http://library.fgcu.edu/Conferences/infostrategies/presentations/2001/holmer.htm.

Horn, Judy. "The Future Is Now: Reference Service for the Electronic Era." Paper presented at Crossing the Divide: Proceedings of the Tenth National Conference of the Association of College and Research Libraries, Denver, Colo., 15–18 March 2001. Available at http://www.ala.org/acrl/papers01/horn.pdf.

Hoskisson, Tam, and Deleyne Wentz. "Simplifying Electronic Reference: A Hybrid Approach to One-on-One Consultation." *College and Undergraduate Libraries* 8, no. 2 (2001): 89–102.

Huling, Nancy. "R/Evolution in Reference Services: Research on Digital Reference." *Alki* 16, no. 2 (July 2000): 21–22.

Hulshof, Robert. "Providing Services to Virtual Patrons." *Information Outlook* (January 1999). Available at http://www.sla.org/pubs/serial/io/1999/jan99/hulshof.html.

Jackson, Michael Gordon. "A Primary Knowledge Revolution: New Demands, New Responsibilities for Reference Librarians (A Review Article)." *Library Quarterly* 72, no. 1 (January 2002): 123–28.

Janes, Joseph. "Digital Reference: Reference Librarians' Experiences and Attitudes." *Journal of the American Society for Information Science and Technology* 53, no. 7 (May 2002): 549–66.

———. "Digital Reference: Services, Attitudes, and Evaluation." *Internet Research* 10, no. 3 (2000): 256–58.

———. "Digital Reference Services in Public and Academic Libraries." In *Evaluating Networked Information Services: Techniques, Policy, and Issues,* edited by Charles McClure and John Carlo Bertot. Silver Spring, Md.: American Society for Information Science, 2001.

———. *Introduction to Reference Work in the Digital Age.* New York: Neal-Schuman, 2002.

———. "Live Reference: Too Much Too Fast?" *NetConnect* (supplement to *Library Journal*) (fall 2002): 12–14.

Janes, Joseph, Chrystie Hill, and Alex Rolfe. "Ask-an-Expert Services Analysis." *Journal of the American Society for Information Science and Technology* 52, no. 13 (November 2001): 1106–21.

Jaworowski, Carlene. "There's More to Chat than Chit-Chat: Using Chat Software for Library Instruction." Paper presented at Information Strategies 2001, Fort Myers, Fla., 14–16 November 2001. Available at http://library.fgcu.edu/Conferences/infostrategies/presentations/2001/jaworowski.htm.

Jesudason, Melba. "Outreach to Student-Athletes through E-Mail Reference Service." *Reference Services Review* 28, no. 3 (2000): 262–68.

Johnson, Cameron A., and Laura McCarty. "Distance Education and Digital Reference: The Yellow Brick Road?" *Alki* 17, no. 1 (March 2001): 6–9.

Jonsby, E. "The Virtual Librarian Answers Your Questions." *Scandinavian Public Library Quarterly* 33, no. 3 (2000): 20–22.

Joshi, Ish. "Askusquestions.com—Live Experienced Librarians Available over the Web." *Unabashed Librarian* 118 (2001): 9–12.

Kasowitz, Abby. "Trends and Issues in Digital Reference Services." *ERIC Digest* (November 2001). Available at http://www.ericit.org/digests/EDO-IR-2001-07.shtml.

Kasowitz, Abby, Blythe Bennett, and R. David Lankes. "Quality Standards for Digital Reference Consortia." *Reference and User Services Quarterly* 39, no. 4 (summer 2000): 355–64.

Kawakami, Alice K. "Delivering Digital Reference." *NetConnect* (supplement to *Library Journal*) (spring 2002): 28–29. Available at http://libraryjournal.reviewsnews.com/index.asp?layout=article&articleid=CA210717.

Kenney, Brian. "Live, Digital Reference: A Close Look at Libraries' Exciting New Service. (An LJ Round Table)." *Library Journal* 127, no. 16 (October 2002): 46–50.

Kibbee, Jo, David Ward, and Wei Ma. "Virtual Reference, Real Data: Results of a Pilot Study." *Reference Services Review* 30, no. 1 (2002): 25–36.

Kimmel, Stacey, and Jenne Heise. "Being There: Tools for Online Synchronous Reference." *Online* 25, no. 6 (November/December 2001): 30–39.

Kisby, Cynthia, et al. "Extended Reference Service in the Electronic Environment." *Information Technology and Libraries* 18, no. 2 (June 1999): 92–95.

Kolandaisamy, Matilda, and Malcolm Keech. "Moving Towards 24-Hour Support." Paper presented at the 10th Victorian Association for Library Automation Biennial Conference and Exhibition, Melbourne, Australia, 16–18 February 2000. Available at http://www.vala.org.au/vala2000/2000pdf/Kol_Kee.PDF.

Koyama, Janice T. "http://digiref.scenarios.issues." *Reference and User Services Quarterly* 38, no. 1 (fall 1998): 51–53.

Kresh, Diane Nester. "From Sshh to Search Engine: Reference.net on the World Wide Web." *Information Technology and Libraries* 20, no. 3 (September 2001): 139–42.

———. "Offering High Quality Reference Service on the Web: The Collaborative Digital Reference Service (CDRS)." *D-Lib Magazine* 6, no. 6 (June 2000). Available at http://www.dlib.org/dlib/june00/kresh/06kresh.html.

Lankes, R. David. "The Birth Cries of Digital Reference." *Reference and User Services Quarterly* 39, no. 4 (Summer 2000): 352–54.

———. "Current Status and Future Directions for Digital Reference." Paper presented at Building the Virtual Reference Desk in a 24/7 World, Library of Congress, Washington, D.C., 12 January 2001. Available at http://www.loc.gov/rr/digiref/webcasts/lankes/ lankes.html.

Lankes, R. David, and Pauline Shostack. "The Necessity of Real Time: Fact and Fiction in Digital Reference Systems." *Reference and User Services Quarterly* 41, no. 4 (summer 2002): 350–55.

Lankes, R. David, John W. Collins III, and Abby S. Kasowitz, eds. *Digital Reference Service in the New Millennium: Planning, Management, and Evaluation.* New Library Series, no. 6. New York: Neal-Schuman, 2000.

Lessick, Susan. "Interactive Reference Services (IRS) at UC Irvine: Expanding Reference Services beyond the Reference Desk." Paper presented at the 1997 ACRL Annual Conference, Nashville, Tenn., 11–14 April 1997. Available at http://www.ala.org/acrl/paperhtm/a10.html.

Leveen, Thomas A. "Reference Librarians Chat It Up Online." *Today's Librarian* (May 2001). Available at http://www.todayslibrarian.com/articles/151Feat1.html.

Lindbloom, Mary-Carol. "Ready for Reference: Academic Libraries Offer Live Web-Based Reference: An Analysis of July–December 2001 Activity." 27 March 2002. Available at http://www.alliancelibrarysystem.com/projects/readyref/FallStats.doc.

———. "Ready for Reference: Academic Libraries Offer Live Web-Based Reference. Final Narrative Report (on LSTA-Funded Project)." 2001. Available at http://www.alliancelibrarysystem.com/projects/readyref/FinalReport.doc.

Lipow, Anne Grodzins. "'In Your Face' Reference Service." *Library Journal* 124, no. 13 (August 1999): 50–52.

———. "Reference Service in a Digital Age." *Reference and User Services Quarterly* 38, no. 1 (1998): 47–48.

———. "Serving the Remote User: Reference Service in the Digital Environment." Keynote address at the Ninth Australasian Information Online and On Disc Conference and Exhibition, Sydney, Australia, 19–21 January 1999. Available at http://www.csu.edu.au/special/online99/proceedings99/200.htm/.

———. *The Virtual Reference Librarian's Handbook*. New York: Neal-Schuman, 2002.

Lo Bianco, Nicky, and Colin Vivian. "Creating Canberra's Virtual Community Library Service." Paper presented at 1999 & Beyond: Partnerships & Paradigms (Program of the Reference & Information Services Section of the Australian Library and Information Association), 6 September 1999. Available at http://www.csu.edu.au/special/raiss99/papers/cvivian/.

MacAdam, Barbara, and Suzanne Gray. "A Management Model for Digital Reference Services in Large Institutions." Paper presented at Facets of Digital Reference Service: The Virtual Reference Desk Second Annual Digital Reference Conference, Seattle, Wash., 16–17 October 2000. Available at http://www.vrd.org/conferences/VRD2000/proceedings/macadam-gray1-01.shtml.

Marsteller, Matt, and Paul Neuhaus. "The Chat Reference Experience at Carnegie Mellon University." Paper presented at the American Library Association Annual Conference, San Francisco, Calif., June 2001. Available at http://www.contrib.andrew.cmu.edu/~matthewm/ALA_2001_chat.html.

Mathews, Brian, et al. "Real-Time Reference Round-up." Paper presented at Information Strategies 2001, Fort Myers, Fla., 14–16 November 2001. Available at http://library.fgcu.edu/Conferences/infostrategies/presentations/2001/viggiano.htm.

Maxwell, Nancy Kalikow. "Establishing and Maintaining Live Online Reference Service." *Library Technology Reports* 38, no. 4 (July/August 2002): 3–78.

McClennen, Michael, and Patricia Memmott. "Roles in Digital Reference." *Information Technology and Libraries* 20, no. 3 (September 2001): 143–48. Available at http://www.lita.org/ital/2003_mcclennan.html/.

McClure, Charles R., and R. David Lankes. "Assessing Quality in Digital Reference Services: A Research Prospectus." Information Institute of Syracuse, 2001. Available at http://quartz.syr.edu/quality/Overview.htm.

McGill, Lou. "Global Chat: Web-Based Enquiries at the University of Leicester." In *Libraries without Walls 4: The Delivery of Library Services to Distant Users,* edited by Peter Brophy, Shelagh Fisher, and Zoë Clarke, 87–98. London: Facet, 2002.

McGlamery, Susan. "Creating a Consortial Chat and Collaborative Browsing Service." Paper presented at Building the Virtual Reference Desk in a 24/7 World, Library of Congress, Washington, D.C., 12 January 2001. Available at http://www.loc.gov/rr/digiref/webcasts/mcglamery/mcglamery.html.

McGlamery, Susan, and Steve Coffman. "Moving Reference to the Web." *Reference and User Services Quarterly* 39, no. 4 (summer 2000): 380–86.

McKinzie, Steve, and Jonathon D. Lauer. "Virtual Reference: Overrated, Inflated, and Not Real." *Charleston Advisor* 4, no. 2 (October 2002). Available at http://www.charlestonco.com/features.cfm?id=112&type=ed.

McLaren, Scott. "Virtual Reference: A Tired Idea Already?" *The Courier* (journal of the Toronto Chapter of the Special Libraries Association) 38, no. 4 (summer 2001). Available at http://www.sla.org/chapter/ctor/courier/v38/v38n4a5.htm.

Meloche, Joseph A. "The Importance of Digital Reference in Supporting Critical Thinking in Distance Education." Paper presented at Facets of Digital Reference Service: The Virtual Reference Desk Second Annual Digital Reference Conference, Seattle, Wash., 16–17 October 2000. Available at http://www.vrd.org/conferences/VRD2000/proceedings/Meloche12-14.shtml.

Meola, Marc, and Sam Stormont. "Real-Time Reference Service for the Remote User: From the Telephone and Electronic Mail to Internet Chat, Instant Messaging, and Collaborative Software." *Reference Librarian* 67/68 (1999): 29–40.

———. *Starting and Operating Live Virtual Reference Services: A How-to-Do-It Manual for Librarians*. New York: Neal-Schuman, 2002.

Missingham, Roxanne. "Virtual Reference: Online Questions and Answers." *Gateways* 49 (February 2001). Available at http://www.nla.gov.au/ntwkpubs/gw/49/p19a01.html.

———. "Virtual Services for Virtual Readers: Reference Reborn in the E-Library." Paper presented at Capitalising on Knowledge: The Information Profession in the 21st Century, Annual Conference of the Australian Library and Information Association, Canberra, Australia, 23–26 October 2000. Available at http://www.alia.org.au/conferences/alia2000/proceedings/roxanne.missingham.html.

Mon, L. "Digital Reference Service." *Government Information Quarterly* 17, no. 3 (2000): 309–18.

Moyo, L. M. "Reference Anytime Anywhere: Towards Virtual Reference Services at Penn State." *Electronic Library* 20, no. 1 (2002): 22–28.

Oder, Norman. "The Shape of E-Reference." *Library Journal* 126, no. 2 (February 2001): 46–50.

Olkowski, Stacy. "Ask a Librarian Live: Using Chat Technology to Expand Remote Reference Services in an Academic Business Library." Paper presented at the SLA Annual Conference, San Antonio, Tex., 13 June 2001.

O'Neill, Nancy. "Digital Reference in a Public Library." Paper presented at Building the Virtual Reference Desk in a 24/7 World, Library of Congress, Washington, D.C., 12 January 2001. Available at http://www.loc.gov/rr/digiref/webcasts/oneill/oneill.html.

———. "E-Mail Reference Service in the Public Library: A Virtual Necessity." *Public Libraries* 38, no. 5 (September/October 1999): 302–3, 305.

Ormes, Sarah. "Public Libraries Corner: Ask a Librarian." *Ariadne* 13 (January 1998). Available at http://www.ariadne.ac.uk/issue13/public-libraries/.

Parsons, Anne Marie. "Digital Reference: How Libraries Can Compete with Aska Services." *Digital Library Federation Newsletter* 2, no. 1 (January 2001). Available at http://www.diglib.org/pubs/news02_01/RefBenchmark.htm.

Patrick, Susan, and Cathy Matthews. "Ask a Librarian LIVE." *College and Research Libraries News* 63, no. 4 (April 2002): 280–81.

Patterson, Rory. "Live Virtual Reference: More Work and More Opportunity." *Reference Services Review* 29, no. 3 (2001): 204–9.

Payne, Georgina, and David Bradbury. "The OPAL Project: Developing an Automated Online Reference System for Distance Learners." *D-Lib Magazine* 7, no. 6 (June 2001). Available at http://www.dlib.org/dlib/june01/06inbrief.html.

Peters, Thomas A. "Current Opportunities for the Effective Meta-Assessment of Online Reference Services." *Library Trends* 49, no. 2 (fall 2000): 334–49.

Powell, Carol A., and Pamela S. Bradigan. "E-Mail Reference Services: Characteristics and Effects on Overall Reference Services at an Academic Health Sciences Library." *Reference and User Services Quarterly* 41, no. 2 (winter 2001): 170–78.

Quint, Barbara. "The Digital Library of the Future: CrossRef Search and QuestionPoint Offer Challenges to Traditional Services." *Information Today* 19, no. 7 (July/August 2002): 8, 10, 12.

———. "QuestionPoint Marks New Era in Virtual Reference." *Information Today* (10 June 2002). Available at http://www.infotoday.com/newsbreaks/nb020610-1.htm.

Regan, Caroline. "Virtual Reference: 24 x 7 in Your Library/Information Centre." *Online Currents* 16, no. 2 (March 2001). Available at http://www.sofcom.com.au/olc/Sample.html.

Richardson, Joanna, et al. "'Ask a Librarian' Electronic Reference Services: The Importance of Corporate Culture, Communication and Service Attitude." Paper presented at AusWeb2K, the Sixth Australian World Wide Web Conference, Cairns, Australia, 12–17 June 2000. Available at http://www.bond.edu.au/library/jpr/ausweb2k/.

Roberts, Helen. "Any Time, Any Place: Virtual Reference Services." *Australian Academic and Research Libraries* 31, no. 4 (December 2000).

Roberts, Lisa. "Choosing a Chat Reference Software Solution: The Devil Is in the Details." Paper presented at Information Strategies 2001, Fort Myers, Fla., 14–16 November 2001. Available at http://library.fgcu.edu/Conferences/infostrategies/presentations/2001/roberts.htm.

Rockman, Ilene F. "Internet Speed, Library Know-How Intersect in Digital Reference." In *The Bowker Annual: Library and Book Trade Almanac*. 47th ed. Edited by Dave Bogart and Julia C. Blixrud, 234–48. Medford, N.J.: Information Today, 2002.

———. "Visionary Pragmatism in an E-Library Environment." *Reference Services Review* 29, no. 3 (2001): 169–70.

Ronan, Jana. "Virtual Reference: A Hot New Idea for Extending Services to Remote Users." *LIRT News* (September 2000). Available at http://web.uflib.ufl.edu/instruct/LIRT/2000/schat.html.

Ruppel, Margie, and Jody Condit Fagan. "Instant Messaging Reference: Users' Evaluation of Library Chat." *RSR: Reference Services Review* 30, no. 3 (August 2002): 183–97.

Ryder, M. A., and B. Nebeker. "Implementing an 'Ask a Librarian' Electronic Reference Service." *Community and Junior College Libraries* 9, no. 1 (1999): 21–34.

Schneider, Karen G. "The Distributed Librarian: Live, Online, Real-Time Reference." *American Libraries* 31, no. 11 (November 2000): 64. Available at http://www.ala.org/alonline/netlib/il1100.html.

———. "My Patron Wrote Me a Letter: The Joy of E-Mail Reference." *American Libraries* 31, no. 1 (January 2000): 96. Available at http://www.ala.org/alonline/netlib/il100.html.

Schwartz, Jennifer. "Digital Reference at Bobst Library." *Connect Magazine* (fall 2001). Available at http://www.nyu.edu/its/connect/01fall/pdfs/schwartz.pdf.

Sears, JoAnn. "Chat Reference Service: An Analysis of One Semester's Data." *Issues in Science and Technology Librarianship,* no. 32 (fall 2001). Available at http://www.istl.org/istl/01-fall/article2.html.

Silverstein, Joanne. "A Study of Digital Reference in a Federal Agency." *Update: Semiannual Bulletin of the ERIC Clearinghouse on Information and Technology* 21, no. 3 (spring 2001). Available at http://www.ericit.org/docs/silverstein.shtml.

Sloan, Bernie. "Electronic Reference Services: Some Suggested Guidelines." *Reference and User Services Quarterly* 38 (summer 1998): 77–81. Available at http://www.lis.uiuc.edu/~b-sloan/guide.html.

———. "Ready for Reference: Academic Libraries Offer Live Web-Based Reference. Evaluating System Use. Final Report." 11 July 2001. Available at http://www.lis.uiuc.edu/~b-sloan/r4r.final.htm.

———. "Ready for Reference: Academic Libraries Offer Live Web-Based Reference. Preliminary Report." 25 May 2001. Available at http://www.lis.uiuc.edu/~b-sloan/ready4ref.htm.

———. "Service Perspectives for the Digital Library: Remote Reference Services." *Library Trends* 47 (summer 1998): 117–43. Available at http://www.lis.uiuc.edu/~b-sloan/e-ref.html. (Pre-publication version.)

Smith, Rhonda M., Stephanie F. Race, and Meredith Ault. "Virtual Desk: Real Reference." *Journal of Library Administration* 32, no. 1/2 (2001): 371–82.

Sonnenwald, Diane H., et al. "Collaboration Services in a Participatory Digital Library: An Emerging Design." 1999. Available at http://www.ils.unc.edu/ils/research/reports/TR-2001-03.pdf.

Stacey-Bates, Kristine K. "Ready-Reference Resources and E-Mail Reference on Academic ARL Web Sites." *Reference and User Services Quarterly* 40, no. 1 (fall 2000): 61–73.

Stahl, Joan R. "CDRS at the Smithsonian Art Museum." Online Computer Library Center. Available at http://www2.oclc.org/oclc/pdf/printondemand/cdrssmithsonian.pdf.

Stahl, Joan R., and Diane Kresh. "Online, Virtual, E-Mail, Digital, Real Time: The Next Generation of Reference Services." *Art Documentation* 20, no. 1 (2001): 26–30.

Stanley, Deborah, and Natasha Lyandres. "Reference Assistance to Remote Users." *Reference Librarian* 73 (2001): 243–52.

Stemper, James A., and John T. Butler. "Developing a Model to Provide Digital Reference Services." *Reference Services Review* 29, no. 3 (2001): 172–88.

Steury, Tim. "Encouraging Online Questioners to Question Their Questions." Paper presented at Facets of Digital Reference Service: The Virtual Reference Desk Second Annual Digital Reference Conference, Seattle, Wash., 16–17 October 2000. Available at http://www.vrd.org/conferences/VRD2000/proceedings/steuryfinal.shtml.

Stormont, Sam. "Going Where the Users Are: Live Digital Reference." *Information Technology and Libraries* 20, no. 3 (September 2001): 129–34.

———. "Here, There, and Everywhere—Live Virtual Reference." *Collection Management* 26, no. 2 (2001): 79–87.

———. "Interactive Reference Project: Assessment after Two Years." Paper presented at Facets of Digital Reference Service: The Virtual Reference Desk Second Annual Digital Reference Conference, Seattle, Wash., 16–17 October 2000. Available at http://www.vrd.org/conferences/VRD2000/proceedings/stormont.shtml.

Straw, Joseph E. "A Virtual Understanding: The Reference Interview and Question Negotiation in the Digital Age." *Reference and User Services Quarterly* 39, no. 4 (summer 2000): 376–79.

Tarlton, Martha, and Monika Antonelli. "Real Time Virtual Reference at the University of North Texas." *Proceedings of the Consortium of College and University Media Centers 2000 Annual Conference* (2000): 183–92. Available at http://www.indiana.edu/~ccumc/tarlton.pdf.

Tennant, Roy. "Of Human and Humane Assistance." *Library Journal* 124 (June 1999): 30.

Tenopir, Carol. "Virtual Reference Services in a Real World." *Library Journal* 126, no. 12 (July 2001): 38–40.

Tomaiuolo, Nicholas G. "Aska and You May Receive: Commercial Reference Services on the Web." *Searcher* 8, no. 5 (May 2001): 56–63.

Tomaiuolo, Nicholas G., and Joan Garrett Packer. "Aska Do's, Don'ts and How-To's: Lessons Learned in a Library." *Searcher* 8, no. 3 (March 2000): 32–35.

Trump, Judith F., and Ian P. Tuttle. "Here, There, and Everywhere: Reference at the Point-of-Need." *Journal of Academic Librarianship* 27, no. 6 (November 2001): 464–66.

Tyckoson, David. "On the Desirableness of Personal Relations between Librarians and Readers: The Past and Future of Reference Service." RUSA Forum on the Future of Reference Services, 2002. Available at http://www.ala.org/rusa/forums/tyckoson_forum.html.

Ware, Susan A. "Interactive Reference at a Distance: A Corporate Model for Academic Libraries." *Reference Librarian* 69/70 (summer 2000): 171–79.

Wasik, Joann M. "Asking the Experts: Digital Reference and the Virtual Reference Desk." *D-Lib Magazine* 6, no. 5 (May 2000). Available at http://www.dlib.org/dlib/may00/05inbrief.html#WASIK.

———. "Information Professionals Chart Future of Internet Q&A." *Update: Semiannual Bulletin of the ERIC Clearinghouse on Information and Technology* 21, no. 3 (spring 2001). Available at http://www.ericit.org/docs/wasik.shtml.

West, Jessamyn. "Information for Sale: My Experience with Google Answers." *Searcher* 10, no. 9 (October 2002). Available at http://www.infotoday.com/searcher/oct02/west.htm.

White, Marilyn Domas. "Diffusion of an Innovation: Digital Reference Service in Carnegie Foundation Master's Academic Institution Libraries." *Journal of Academic Librarianship* 27, no. 3 (May 2001): 173–87.

———. "Digital Reference Services—Framework for Analysis and Evaluation." *Library and Information Science Research* 23, no. 3 (autumn 2001): 211–31.

Whitlatch, Jo Bell. "Reference Futures: Outsourcing, the Web, or Knowledge Counseling." RUSA Forum on the Future of Reference Services, 2002. Available at http://www.ala.org/rusa/forums/whitlatch_forum.html.

Witten, Shelle. "Being RAD: Reference at a Distance in a Multi-Campus Institution." In *The Tenth Off-Campus Library Services Conference Proceedings: Cincinnati, Ohio, April 17–19, 2002,* edited by Patrick B. Mahoney, 423–38. Mount Pleasant, Mich.: Central Michigan University, 2002.

INDEX

A
Adler, Kerry, 8
Administration software interface, 134–37
Advertising. *See* Marketing plan
AllExperts, 8
Alliance Library System, 28
AltaVista, 4
America Online (AOL), 3
Answers, 93
Application procedure (sample), 55–58
Ask a Librarian, 9, 79
Ask Jeeves, 4, 8–9, 93
AskShamu, 79
Association of Research Libraries (ARL), 4–5
Authentication of patrons, 112

B
"Back" communications channel, 71
Banners, 83
Benchmark Portal, 92
Bibliographic instruction (online), 23–24, 83
Bookmarks/premiums, 82, 130–31

C
Call volume, 36–41, 63–64
Casey, Terry, 5–7
CDRS Network. *See* Collaborative Digital Reference Service (CDRS)
Chat programs
  adapting software from, 34
  future of, 93
  proactive, 81–82
  reference and, 15–18
Clevenet, 26, 28, 63
Collaborative Digital Reference Service (CDRS), 10, 12
Collaborative reference
  application sharing, 118–20, 122–23
  co-browsing, 117, 120–23
  copyright and, 42–43
  historical efforts of, 10–14
  to lower costs, 47
  planning for, 28–30
  usage and, 91
Colorado Community College, 2
Columbus (Ohio) Public Library Board, 5–7
Competency, 61–62
Consortiums, 28–30. *See also* Collaborative reference
Copyright, 42–43, 124–25
Cornell University, 19
Costs
  chat programs and, 18
  collaborative services and, 29
  fee-based services and, 94
  marketing, 46–47
  marketing to non-users of library and, 85
  off-site virtual reference and, 52
  outsourcing of reference services and, 27
  reference services and, 45–46
  resource/development, 46

Costs (cont'd)
- of software, 33, 45
- staffing and, 41, 46
- of web contact center software, 19–20

Cyberatlas, 96

D

Desktop operations and videoconferencing, 14
Dig-Ref, 33
DirectHit, 4
Disabled patrons, 109
Downloads, 108

E

E-commerce companies
- adapting software from, 34
- learning from experiences of, 95
- proactive chat and, 81–82
- web contact center software and, 18–19

E-mail
- impact of, 9–13
- as session transcripts, 124

Eglobal Library, 26
Employment
- application procedure (sample), 55–58
- screening test (appendix B), 146–55

Equipment. *See also* Software
- chat programs and, 15–16
- desktop videoconferencing and, 14–15
- hardware, 46, 59

Erlang, Agner Krarup, 37
Erlang C formula, 37–41
Ethics of customer service, 59–60
Evaluations
- customer satisfaction and, 64–65
- satisfaction surveys (appendix A), 129
- service statistics and, 63–64
- staff performance/reference transcripts and, 65–70
- transcript analysis tools, 125

ExpertNet, 8

F

FAST, 4
Feature set of software, 31–32
Fee-based services, 94
Fiander, Michelle, 49
File sharing, 117
"Follow-the-sun" collaboratives, 29
Foreign-language reference, 98–99
Form sharing, 118
Francoeur, Stephen, 17, 20, 33

G

Google, 4, 9, 89
Google Answers, 94
GoTo, 4
Green, Samuel Swett, 1–3, 48
Groopz, 81

H

Hardware, 46, 59
Henshall, Kay, 49
HumanClick, 16

I

Information Institute of Syracuse, 10
Inforocket, 8
Inktomi, 4
Instant messaging programs
- back channel and, 71
- future aspects of, 97
- as interactive service, 15–18
- patron access and, 109

Internet
- marketing and, 74
- off-site costs and, 52
- outside links as marketing technique, 88–89
- reference services and, 3–7

Internet Public Library (IPL), 10–11

J

James J. Hill Reference Library (St. Paul, Minnesota), 24, 100
Jupiter Communications, 96

K

Keen, 8
King County Library System, 51, 103

KnowItNow
- collaborative services and, 28
- marketing and, 79
- patron interface and, 44
- publicity and, 86
- training and, 63
- as turnkey service, 26

L

Lands End, 95
Librarians. *See also* Staff
- communication with patrons (appendix A), 112–16, 118
- e-mail reference and, 10–13
- multiple patrons and, 130
- queuing/routing structure of software and (appendix A), 141–44
- sample pre-employment screening test (appendix B), 146–55
- and software interface (appendix A), 129–32
- and training/support (appendix A), 133–34
- as volunteers, 47

Libraries
- as information source, 1
- reference trend away from, 4–6
- staff scheduling in, 11

Library of Congress (LC)
- Collaborative Digital Reference Service (CDRS) of, 10
- e-mail reference and, 12

Library programming, 83
Library Systems and Services, LLC (LSSI)
- Erlang C formula and, 37–41
- management of virtual reference at, 49, 52
- reference transcript evaluation form, 68–70
- sample application procedure at, 55–58
- sample pre-employment screening test of (appendix B), 146–55
- turnkey services and, 26
- usage according to, 91
- web contact center software and, 20
- Web Reference Center, 52, 55–57, 146–47

Library-to-library reference services, 24–25. *See also* Collaborative reference
Licensed or hosted software. *See* Software
Links, 88–89
Live interaction software, 18–20
LivePerson, 19, 81
LiveRef, 17, 20, 33
Livereference, 33
Location of virtual reference, 49–53
Log-in screens, 43–44
LookSmart, 93
LSSI. *See* Library Systems and Services, LLC

M

Marketing plan
- costs of, 46–47
- existing library users and, 78–84
- Internet and, 74
- to non-users of library, 84–89
- patron interface and, 44

McKiernan, Gerry, 18, 20, 33
Media features/columns, 87–88
Mentoring, 62
Metropolitan Cooperative Library System, 20
MOO. *See* Multiuser object-oriented environments (MOOs)
Multiuser object-oriented environments (MOOs), 13–15

N

National Center for Education Statistics, 21 n1
NDP Group New Media Search Satisfaction Survey, 7
NetEffect, 19
New York Public Library (NYPL), 98–99

O

Office hours (online), 23
Online Computer Library Center (OCLC), 1
Online databases
- as reference source, 2–3
- as resources, 43

Online programs, 87, 128
Operating system requirements, 59, 109
Outsourcing reference services
  collaborative services as, 30
  planning for, 26–27
  subject specialists and, 99–100

P
Page pushing, 117
Patrons
  characteristics of virtual reference librarian and, 54
  collaborative services and, 29
  costs to, 46
  customer service ethic, 59–60
  disabled, 109
  downloading chat programs, 17–18
  evaluation of satisfaction, 64–65
  interfacing with, 43–44
  marketing plan for, 78–84
  marketing to non-users of library, 84–89
  multiple, 130
  profiling of (appendix A), 126–28
  queuing/routing structure of software and (appendix A), 141–44
  service hours and, 75–76
  service policies and, 42
  and software requirements (appendix A), 108–12
  and time on hold, 38–39
Persistent button feature, 80–81
Planning/designing systems. *See also* Marketing plan
  choosing staff, 35–36
  collaboration with others for, 28–30
  do-it-yourself model, 25–26
  marketing and, 44
  purchase of, 26–27
  setting goals and, 22–25
  software, 31–34
Policies
  refresher training on, 63
  service, 42, 75
Preferred Solutions Call Center Directory, 39
Privacy
  instant messaging software and, 18
  proactive chat and, 81–82
Programming (online), 24
Proxy server co-browsing, 122
Publicity, 85–88. *See also* Marketing plan

Q
QandACafe, 44
QandANJ
  collaborative services and, 28
  marketing and, 79
  publicity and, 86
Quality of collaborative services, 30

R
Ready for Reference, 28
Reference
  commercial web services, 7–9
  costs of, 45–46
  foreign-language, 98–99
  future of reference desk, 101–4
  and interview/questions (appendix B), 146–55
  library-to-library, 24–25
  subject specialists and, 99–100
  transcripts, 65–70
  via e-mail, 9–13
Request for proposal (RFP), 34
Resources
  characteristics of virtual reference librarian and, 54–55
  content sharing of (appendix A), 116–20
  costs of, 46
  database co-browsing of (appendix A), 120–23
  online, 43
  and training of staff, 59–60, 63
Resume/cover letters, 55–56
Routine mailings/correspondence, 83

S
Salaries, 8
Sample pre-employment screening test (appendix B), 146–55
ScheduleSource, 71

Scheduling
  availability and, 57
  choosing staff and, 35–36
  Erlang C formula for calculation of staff, 37–41
  service hours and, 75–76
  using software for, 70–71
Screenshots, 116–17
Search Engine Watch, 4, 21 n1
Search engines. *See also specific search engines, i.e.,* Google
  fee-based services and, 94
  linking to, 89
  searches per year, 4
Service policies, 42, 75
Session transcripts (appendix A), 124–26
Slide shows, 117
Software
  characteristics of virtual reference librarian and, 54, 57–58
  for chat programs, 16–18
  choosing, 31–34
  collaboration of, 93
  competency of staff using, 61–62
  costs of, 45
  for desktop videoconferencing, 14–15
  limited usage and, 92–93
  online programming and, 24
  for outside links as marketing technique, 88
  privacy issues of, 18
  for scheduling, 70–71
  telephone reference centers and, 50–52
  training of staff on, 58, 60, 62
  web contact center software, 18–20
Software feature checklist (appendix A)
  access by patron, 110–11
  administration, 134–37
  communication, 112–16
  content sharing, 116–20
  customization, 144–45
  database co-browsing, 120–23
  librarian's interface, 129–32
  licensed or hosted, 138–40
  online meetings, 128
  patron authentication, 112
  patron profiling, 126–28
  patron requirements, 108–10
  queuing/routing structure, 141–44
  satisfaction surveys, 129
  session transcripts, 124–26
  training/support/documentation of librarians, 133–34
South Jersey Regional Library Cooperative, 28
Staff. *See also* Scheduling
  access to subject specialists and, 99–100
  "back" communications channel and, 71
  calculating for number of, 36–37, 41
  characteristics of virtual reference librarian, 53–55
  choosing, 35–36
  costs of, 46
  evaluations of performance, 65–70
  future of reference desk and, 101–4
  location of virtual reference and, 49–53
  off-site, 52–53
  online programming and, 24
  outsourcing of reference services and, 26–27
  sample application procedure, 55–58
  sample pre-employment screening test (appendix B), 146–55
  shared through collaborative services, 29–30
  training of, 58–63
Subject specialists, 99–100
Subscription-based services, 24

T

Teaching Librarian, 17, 20, 33
Telecommuting. *See* Location of virtual reference
Telephone reference, 2, 50–51
Training for staff
  mentoring, 62
  online practice as, 61–62
  online programming and, 23–24, 83
  support/documentation and (appendix A), 133–34
  virtual reference software, 58, 60

Transcripts (appendix A), 124–26
Turnkey services, 26–27
24/7 Reference, 29
24/7 reference service, 75–76

U

University of Calgary, 19
University of California at Irvine (UCI), 14
URL-pushing co-browsing, 121
Usage. *See also* Patrons
  collaborative services and, 29
  future of reference desk and, 102–3
  limited, 91–93
  of major messaging services, 96
  planning for call volume, 36–41

V

Vendors. *See also* Collaborative reference
  licensed or hosted (appendix A), 138–40
  request for proposal (RFP) and, 34
Videoconferencing, 14
Virtual reality
  chat programs and, 15–18
  multiuser object-oriented environments (MOOs) and, 13–15
Virtual Reference Desk, 10
Voice over Internet Protocol, 16, 113

W

"Warm transfer" capabilities, 142
Web contact center software, 18–20
Web Reference Center. *See* Library Systems and Services, LLC
WebHelp, 7–8, 93
WebWizards, 7–8
Welcome packages, 83
World Wide Web (WWW). *See also specific search engines, i.e.,* Google
  contact center software, 18–19
  Erlang C formula on, 38–39
  usage of, 5–6
  videoconferencing and, 14